CLOSING
THE
RTI GAP

WHY POVERTY **AND** CULTURE **COUNT**

A Joint Publication

Solution Tree | Press a division of Solution Tree naesp™

Donna
Walker Tileston

555 North Morton Street
Bloomington, IN 47404

800.733.6786 (toll free) / 812.336.7700
FAX: 812.336.7790

email: info@solution-tree.com
solution-tree.com

Printed in the United States of America

14 13 12 11 10   1 2 3 4 5

FSC
Mixed Sources
Product group from well-managed
forests and other controlled sources
Cert no. SW-COC-002283
www.fsc.org
© 1996 Forest Stewardship Council

Library of Congress Cataloging-in-Publication Data

Tileston, Donna Walker.
 Closing the RTI gap : why poverty and culture count / Donna Walker Tileston.
    p. cm.
 Includes bibliographical references and index.
 ISBN 978-1-935249-38-2 (perfect-bound) -- ISBN 978-1-935249-39-9 (library binding)
 1. Remedial teaching--Social aspects--United States. 2. Effective teaching--United States. 3. Classroom management--United States. I. Title.

 LB1029.R4.T55 2011
 371.9'043--dc22

                                                    2010027549

Solution Tree
Jeffrey C. Jones, CEO & President

Solution Tree Press
President: Douglas M. Rife
Publisher: Robert D. Clouse
Vice President of Production: Gretchen Knapp
Managing Production Editor: Caroline Wise
Copy Editor: Tara Perkins
Proofreader: Elisabeth Abrams
Text Designer: Amy Shock
Cover Designer: Orlando Angel

Acknowledgments

Thank you, Robb Clouse, for believing in me and my work. Gretchen Knapp: Thank you for your patience and expert advice. A big thanks to Solution Tree for all they do for their authors.

Solution Tree Press would like to thank the following reviewers:

Theresa Austin
Professor, Department of
Teacher Education and
Curriculum Studies
University of Massachusetts
Amherst, Massachusetts

Elizabeth A'Vant
School Psychologist
Providence Schools
Providence, Rhode Island

Jon Bennetts
Fourth-Grade Teacher
Carberry Intermediate School
Emmett, Idaho

Heidi Legg Burross
Clinical Assistant Professor,
Department of Educational
Psychology
University of Arizona
Tucson, Arizona

Cassandra Cole
Director, Center for Education
and Lifelong Learning
Indiana University
Bloomington, Indiana

Mary Hendricks-Harris
Director, Adult Learning and
Program Evaluation
Francis Howell School District
St. Charles, Missouri

Stacey Higgins
Second-Grade Teacher
Ridge Elementary School
Bowling Green, Ohio

Sheri Hunter
Director of Professional
Development
Clinton Central School
District
Clinton, New York

Amy Suzanne Johnson
Assistant Professor, Depart-
ment of Instruction and
Teacher Education
University of South Carolina
Columbia, South Carolina

Angela Mosley
Assistant Principal
Armstrong High School
Richmond, Virginia

Michael Orosco
Assistant Professor, Graduate
School of Education
University of California,
Riverside
Riverside, California

Jean Powell
Response to Intervention
Coordinator
Greenwood School District 50
Greenwood, South Carolina

Tammy Rasmussen
Response to Intervention
Coach
Southern Oregon RTI
Roseburg, Oregon

Sheri Shirley
Principal
Oakland Heights Elementary
School
Russellville, Arkansas

Table of Contents

About the Author

Donna Walker Tileston, EdD, is the founder and president of Strategic Teaching and Learning in Dallas, Texas. Dr. Walker Tileston has written twenty-four books to date. She received the Association of Educational Publishers Distinguished Achievement award in 2005 for her ten-book series, *What Every Teacher Should Know,* and again in 2009 for her book *Why Culture Counts: Teaching Children of Poverty,* which also won the Bronze Award for Book of the Year from *ForeWord* magazine.

She has presented at international, national, and state conferences to thousands of educators and provides training institutes on culture, poverty, and response to intervention.

Introduction

Getting It Right This Time

In the early 1950's, racial segregation in public schools was the norm across America. Although all schools in a given district were supposed to be equal, most black schools were far inferior to their white counterparts.
—Lisa Cozzens

In the 1950s, school segregation was rampant in many states, including Kansas, where Linda Brown lived and went to elementary school in Topeka, the state capital. Because they were African American, Linda Brown and her younger sister, Mary Ann, had to walk through a dangerous switchyard twice a day to get to the bus stop for the ride to their segregated school. A school for white children stood only a mile from Linda's house, but she was denied admittance because of her race.

Most Americans today look back on that time with amazement and chagrin that educated people could ever have thought it was acceptable public policy to put children in danger in order to enforce school segregation. Linda Brown's father did not think it made sense at the time, and it was his drive for justice for his children—and all African American children—that led to the famous *Brown v. Board of Education* case, in which the U.S. Supreme Court decided that separate is not equal. Dr. Hugh W. Speer, an expert witness in the case at the district court level, said:

> If the colored children are denied the experience in
> school of associating with white children, who represent
> 90 percent of our national society in which these colored
> children must live, then the colored child's curriculum is
> being greatly curtailed. The Topeka curriculum or any
> school curriculum cannot be equal under segregation.
> (quoted in Knappman, 1994, p. 467)

That idea was echoed in the Supreme Court case. Chief Justice
Earl Warren read the unanimous decision:

> We come then to the question presented: Does segre-
> gation of children in public schools solely on the basis of
> race, even though the physical facilities and other "tan-
> gible" factors may be equal, deprive the children of the
> minority group of equal educational opportunities? We
> believe that it does. . . . We conclude that in the field of
> public education the doctrine of "separate but equal"
> has no place. Separate educational facilities are inher-
> ently unequal. Therefore, we hold that the plaintiffs and
> others similarly situated for whom the actions have been
> brought are, by reason of the segregation complained
> of, deprived of the equal protection of the laws guaran-
> teed by the Fourteenth Amendment. (quoted in Ziegler,
> 1958, p. 78)

This argument—that separate education is inherently unequal—
was later used by advocates arguing for the rights of a different
group of children: those with disabilities. Prior to 1975, children
with physical or mental impairments were not guaranteed an
education in public schools; schools could reject students with
disabilities on the grounds that they had neither the facilities
nor the expertise to accommodate special needs. Using the same
arguments that had been a part of the *Brown v. Board of Education* (1954) case, advocates argued for the rights of all children to
have a free public education. Of particular importance to these
advocates were the words of the Supreme Court Chief Justice
Earl Warren in the Brown case:

> In these days, it is doubtful that any child may reasonably
> be expected to succeed in life if he is denied the oppor-
> tunity of an education. Such an opportunity, where the

State has undertaken to provide it, is a right that must
be made available to all on equal terms. (quoted in
Ziegler, 1958, p. 78)

The Education for All Handicapped Children Act (EAHCA, Public Law 94-142; sometimes referred to as EHA) was enacted by the United States Congress in 1975. Under this law, any public school that accepted federal funds was required to provide an education to children with physical or mental disabilities. Rather than turning away a child with disabilities, the school would first provide careful screening and evaluation, then create an individual education plan (IEP) outlining how the general educational program would be modified to ensure that the child could be successful in public school.

Though the law passed, it didn't succeed in eliminating achievement gaps or inequality in access to quality education, as we shall discuss in chapter 2. Among other problems, some students were misidentified due to inadequate instruction as needing special education services, other students had to wait too long to receive needed services, and disproportionate numbers of students from certain cultural and ethnic groups were identified as learning disabled. As a result, through the years, the law has undergone many changes. It was renamed the Individuals with Disabilities Education Act (IDEA) in 1990 and amended in 1997. Further major amendments were made when President Bush signed the Individuals with Disabilities Education Improvement Act of 2004, which became law in 2005. It is this 2004 version of IDEA that changed the rules regarding how students are identified and placed into special education services, especially in regard to students with specific learning disabilities. No longer are schools allowed to use the discrepancy model of the past, in which observed gaps between potential intelligence and actual achievement played a significant part in the selection of students for special education services. Today, schools must design an intervention plan that requires a high level of instruction for all students and early intervention before failure. Most design a tiered intervention system that uses assessment and observations to provide early interventions for any student at the first sign of difficulty; progress is closely monitored and increasingly intensive interventions offered until the student either succeeds in learning or is evaluated for a specific learning disability. This new model is called response to intervention, or RTI.

The statute is not the only thing that has changed; much has also changed in the way educators and researchers view learning. We have more research on learning from which to draw, and educators have documented which practices are effective. Education philosophy is now oriented toward a belief that not only *can* all children learn, not only do they *deserve* to learn, but they *must* learn—at a high level.

A commonly understood goal of education is to prepare students for success in the real world. Each generation of teachers going back to the little red schoolhouse has been comprised of individuals who were part instructor and part visionary, as they helped to mold the teaching and learning that were needed for their times. Curriculum and pedagogy have evolved just as society and the needs of society have changed. The little red schoolhouse long ago helped prepare students for an agrarian society evolving into an industrial society. Teachers had the tools to do that, and they passed on to their students the knowledge that was needed. Teachers today are preparing students for a global world, in which those future adults will be competing far beyond the city limits of their own communities. For the first time, students are becoming masters of the tools of the generation—technology—before their teachers. The world outside the little red schoolhouse is changing faster than the world inside it. Allowing students to move through the education system as failures until they either drop out or earn a meaningless certificate has never been acceptable. Today, however, the urgency of the problem has escalated.

My work with an early childhood school that teaches children from high-poverty areas of the city brought *Brown v. Board of Education* back to mind. Many of the children in this school do not speak English when they enroll. Some have been rescued from parts of the world where they were condemned to death as part of ethnic cleansing. One child arrived with scarcely a shirt on his back. He had been marked for death, not because of anything he did or that his parents had done, but simply because he did not match the preferred ethnicity of his home country. The United States has come a long way from the 1950s, yet there is still reason to wonder whether this boy will receive the kind of education that he will need to be successful in our globalized world. Certainly, he will speak English when he enters first grade—this small preK school will make sure of that. But he will have many cultural hurdles to jump to become part of mainstream U.S. society, and he most likely will experience some inequality in his education because his family lives in poverty. For many students living in poverty or coming from cultures different from their community's dominant culture, the old problem of unequal access still prevails.

The Supreme Court decision that gave all children equal access to education in *Brown v. Board of Education* is still relevant today as educators and policymakers look at school achievement gaps through the lenses of NCLB and RTI. While all children theoretically have equal access to education, do they in fact—particularly children from poverty and minority cultures—have equal access to a high-quality education that uses best practices and implements necessary modifications that meet the needs of students from all cultures and all socioeconomic levels? An important study led by the Education Trust and based on the 2004–2005 school year found that separate and unequal are still the norm in many states. The study found that in high-poverty schools teachers tend to have less experience, make less money, and are less likely to be "highly qualified" than their peers in more affluent settings (Education Trust, 2005). In a report on the 2007 state test results for California, Jack O'Connell (2008), State Superintendent of Public Instruction, revealed that something more than poverty was affecting the test results for his state. According to O'Connell, African American and Latino students who did *not* live in poverty scored lower in mathematics than did white students living in poverty (as reported in Mangaliman, 2007). California's results are one indication that differences in test scores between white middle-class students and African American or Hispanic students are not simply a matter of poverty; something else is at work. I believe, as do others, that some minority students become instructional casualties as a result of educators' lack of understanding about how various cultures learn. Our current model of teaching and learning is based largely on a Northern European, white, middle-class ethos, and sadly, it often does leave behind students who do not fit that description. Linda Lane, Deputy Superintendent of the Pittsburgh Public Schools, responded to a study led by Robert Strauss of Carnegie Mellon University on the achievement gap, "Poverty is a factor that affects achievement; however, race is a larger factor" (Wereschagin, 2007, p. 1). In fact, the research appears to indicate that culture almost invariably trumps poverty when looking at the factors necessary for closing achievement gaps (Tileston & Darling, 2009).

The goal of helping all children receive the timely, targeted help they need to succeed is wonderful. Certainly the NCLB legislation and 2004 amendments to IDEA open doors to attaining high achievement for all students. But student achievement is not the only gap that we must fill in order to ensure that RTI will avoid the problems of the past and become the program students need. We have to ask ourselves why we are not succeeding in closing the gap for some students and then become better at providing what they need, on their terms:

> A new model for differentiating instruction must view students from poverty as children with *differences* in culture and value systems, and in the ways they respond to unfavorable conditions in the dominant society—not as children with deficits that need to be "fixed." (Tileston & Darling, 2009, p. 27)

This book deals with some of the critical questions we must answer if we are to fulfill the promises of response to intervention. It will provide examples and explain the importance of specific RTI modifications needed to help close the achievement gaps for students from poverty and different cultures.

Chapter 1 looks at the response to intervention model and why it is an integral part of school improvement. When implemented correctly, RTI provides the means to improve instruction for all students and to intervene early before students have failed. Chapter 2 introduces the reader to the terms *culture*, *poverty*, and *RTI*, and sets the stage for why response to intervention must take into consideration modifications for poverty and culture in the areas of identification, best practices, behavior, and assessment. Chapter 3 examines why the planning phase prior to implementing an RTI model is critical to achieving different results than in the past. The chapter includes a list of preventable mistakes gleaned from the research on earlier intervention models. Chapter 4 outlines the priorities for closing the achievement gap at Tier 1, the first level of response in the RTI model: building relationships, focusing on vocabulary, differentiating instruction, and teaching to reach all self-systems. Chapter 5 explores decision making, progress monitoring, and intervention at Tiers 2 and 3. Finally, an epilogue offers some closing thoughts. In addition, a glossary of terms based on the descriptions recommended in IDEA and other sources is also included (pages 135–138). This glossary will help teachers, administrators, policymakers, and others develop a common language for discussing the RTI model and its implementation.

Now that we have the tools we need, will we finally, as Belinda Williams challenged us in her groundbreaking book *Closing the Achievement Gap* in 1996 and again in 2003:

- Elaborate and distinguish between individual and group differences, as well as between the education goals of improving achievement and closing the gaps;

- Analyze the complexity of achievement gaps among groups; and

- Offer integrated strategies to close those gaps? (2003, p. 2)

The achievement gaps between the majority of students and those living in poverty or from cultural backgrounds that differ from their teachers or the majority culture are real and long-standing. My hope in writing this book is that we will seize this opportunity to close them once and for all.

Chapter one

Understanding the Importance of RTI

As educators and researchers have learned more about how students learn and the instructional practices that have the greatest positive effect on learning, laws have been modified to reflect those perceived best practices. The quest for higher achievement and fewer gaps among groups of students has led legislatures to look for alternatives to the procedures used in the past for identifying children with learning disabilities. Let's examine some of the legislation affecting response to intervention and the policy shifts that have led to the creation of RTI models.

Who Is Responsible for a Child's Education?

The Elementary and Secondary Education Act (ESEA, Public Law 89-10) was enacted in 1965, and the Education for All Handicapped Children Act (EAHCA, Public Law 94-142) was passed in 1975. As the introduction noted, prior to that time, students with disabilities were often turned away from enrolling in public schools under the excuse that schools were not prepared to teach them. These laws gave all children the opportunity to a free and appropriate education and put the burden of providing appropriate modifications on the schools. Over the years, the intent of these laws has been clarified through reauthorization and new legislation, in particular the No Child Left Behind Act of 2001

(NCLB) and the Individuals with Disabilities Education Improvement Act of 2004 (IDEA 2004).

Earlier versions of IDEA were thought of as a special education law, and teachers who specialize in special education were charged to carry out the law's provisions. However, disproportionate numbers of students from poverty and from certain ethnic groups were placed in special education programs, such as those for students with learning disabilities, as we shall discuss throughout this book. The problems in special education placements have led to changes in how students with special needs are identified and have broadened responsibilities for these students—indeed, for all students—to *all* educators.

These laws make clear that the responsibility for ensuring the education of every child, regardless of abilities, race, economic status, and so on, rests squarely on the shoulders of educators, and further, that educator accountability has shifted to the level of the individual student, rather than groups of students. For example, NCLB language includes the goals of "holding schools, local education agencies, and states accountable for improving the academic achievement of all students" and "promoting schoolwide reform and ensuring the access of all children to effective, scientifically-based instructional strategies" (PL 107-100 § 1001[4] and [9], as cited in IDEA Partnership, 2007b). In IDEA 2004, Congress moved "to improve the academic achievement and functional performance of children with disabilities including the use of scientifically based instructional practices, to the maximum extent possible" (20 U.S.C. 1400 [c][5][E], as cited in IDEA Partnership, 2007b). Indeed, RTI and NCLB are united in their dedication to providing a high-quality education to all students. According to the National Research Center on Learning Disabilities, "Utilizing a RTI framework across disciplines as well as grade levels is consistent with NCLB and promotes the idea that schools have an obligation to ensure that *all* students participate in strong instructional programs that support multi-faceted learning" (IDEA Partnership, 2007a).

Adequate yearly progress on achieving the goals of these laws is evaluated not only for the whole school or grade level, but also for subgroups sorted by ethnicity, socioeconomic status, gender, special education placement, English language ability, and so on. Thus, effective implementation of IDEA and NCLB requires that assessments will be free of bias and so will correctly assess what and how well students are learning. It assumes that schools will know best practices and current research on factors that affect students' learning, such as poverty and culture, the factors of most concern to this book, and that teachers will have been trained to use and modify those best practices. In particular, IDEA emphasizes effective instruction that is tied to state standards and delivered by highly qualified teachers, as well as progress monitoring to inform instruction and early intervention rather than waiting for a child to fail before providing services. This model has come to be known as response to intervention or RTI.

What Is RTI?

In general terms, RTI is a process that provides "high quality instruction/intervention matched to student needs and uses learning rates over time and the level of performance of students to inform instructional decisions" (IDEA Partnership, 2007b, p. 8). A more detailed definition comes from the special education consortium, the National Research Center on Learning Disabilities (2007):

> Responsiveness to intervention is an education model that promotes early identification of students who may be at risk for learning difficulties. RTI, which may be *one component* in the process a school uses to determine whether a student has a specific learning disability, often involves tiers of increasingly intense levels of service for students. Most students will thrive in general education classrooms. For those who don't, a second tier will focus additional attention on the academic area in which the child struggles. More tiers may be available for students with greater needs.

From this definition, we glean that response to intervention promotes within schools an attitude that educators believe all of their students can learn and that when they do not learn as would be expected for their age and grade level, educators are ready and able to intervene. Teachers do not wait until failure has occurred before deciding that differentiation or more in-depth teaching must take place. This is a critical attitude because it means that intervention will take place the moment that difficulty is recognized, not after the unit or course is finished and the student has already failed.

Good teachers everywhere intervene on a daily basis when students struggle and often agonize over why typical interventions do not work. The difference in RTI is that for the first time, the education system is being held accountable for empowering teachers to know the best practices and how and when to execute them in their classrooms. It also requires universal testing of all students to determine whether they have the skills necessary for success in the classroom so that any needs can be met before problems arise.

Many teachers are using every tool they have. Yet the huge need for RTI clearly shows that the education system has not done a good job of empowering teachers. As Belinda Williams (2003) says, "Absent that body of knowledge and skills required, the ability of educators across the country to interpret the nature of achievement gaps and address the distinct differences among group achievement patterns is left to chance" (p. 6). Education law is explicit in requiring administration to empower teachers. NCLB describes the obligation of local education agencies (LEAs) to provide training for teachers in early intervening services as follows:

> An LEA will provide training to enable teachers to teach and address the needs of students with different learning styles, particularly students with disabilities, students with special learning needs (including students who are gifted and talented), and students with limited English proficiency; and to improve student behavior in the classroom and identify early and appropriate interventions to help these students. (as cited by National Center for Learning Disabilities, 2010)

Fulfilling the promise of this law will be no small task for schools or for teachers. Let's look at what it will entail.

What Are the Principles Behind RTI?

Response to intervention was born of the basic belief that all kids can learn. When correctly implemented, RTI articulates this principle through individualized screening and planning so that every child has access to high-quality instruction and early intervention.

RTI principles include:

- **Prevention-focused approaches**—A scientifically based, differentiated curriculum with various instructional methods is the norm within the school. Learning or behavioral problems are diagnosed before failure occurs.

- **Interventions grounded in research-based instructional strategies**—According to the IDEA Partnership (2007c), research-based instructional strategies, or best practices, are defined as "curriculum and educational interventions that have been proven to be effective for most students based on scientific study." In RTI, when students struggle and are provided with interventions, those interventions must be proven to be effective by scientific research.

- **Fidelity of implementation**—Fidelity means that an intervention program is implemented according to research findings. In other words, teachers do not merely know the names of the best practices; they have been trained in how to implement them correctly in the classroom. For example, the research of Marzano (2007) shows that cooperative learning has a significant effect on student learning. Many teachers do not use cooperative learning because they say it does not work in their classrooms. But a closer examination of what these teachers implement under the name of cooperative learning often reveals that they are merely grouping. To achieve the effect sizes of the research, a teacher must employ *all* of the processes of cooperative learning, which will be discussed further in this book.

- **Ongoing assessment targeted to the specific skills being taught**—Interventions are then monitored to determine their effectiveness by assessing students on the specific issues being targeted by the intervention.

- **Multitiered system of assessment with increased levels of intensity**—When interventions are not effective, a student moves up to a more intensive level or tier of intervention. Intensity factors to modify across each tier include duration, frequency, and time of interventions; group size; and instructor skill level. Modifying these factors means that educators are more likely to get accurate data and to reach their goals.

- **Explicit decision rules**—An individualized problem-solving model or a standardized intervention protocol is used to assess learners' progress and determine transitions between the intervention tiers.

The Tiered or Pyramid Model

The RTI legislation says that intervention systems developed by schools should include two or more tiers. Though design of the tiers may vary, schools must allow adequate time and use multiple methods of evaluation in the interval between the first signs that intervention may be needed and placement of a student in a special program. Time allows educators to determine whether a child's learning difficulties are caused by systemic deficiencies (ineffective teaching) rather than actual cognitive impairment.

According to Bender and Shores (2007), the most common model for response to intervention is a three-tier model, often referred to as a pyramid because most students are served by the base instruction at Tier 1 and just a few children are served at the tip in Tier 3. According to IDEA 2004, Bender and Shores note:

> Academic and behavioral research support an 80–15–5 model of student learning connected to a comprehensive curriculum with quality teaching strategies and materials being used. In other words, with the implementation of

a comprehensive curriculum with quality teaching strategies and materials . . . , 80% will need at least temporary interventions from time to time, 15% will need more intense interventions at the Tier Two level and 5% will be in need of more intense and individual interventions to support learning at Tier Three. (p. 15)

Figure 1.1 describes the three tiers most often used in schools.

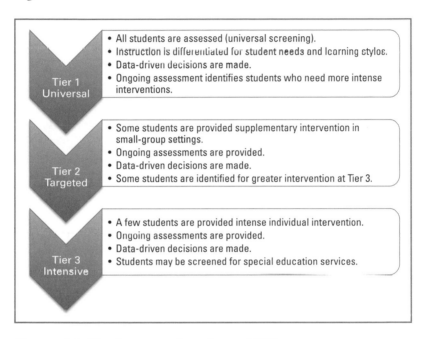

Tier 1 Universal
- All students are assessed (universal screening).
- Instruction is differentiated for student needs and learning styles.
- Data-driven decisions are made.
- Ongoing assessment identifies students who need more intense interventions.

Tier 2 Targeted
- Some students are provided supplementary intervention in small-group settings.
- Ongoing assessments are provided.
- Data-driven decisions are made.
- Some students are identified for greater intervention at Tier 3.

Tier 3 Intensive
- A few students are provided intense individual intervention.
- Ongoing assessments are provided.
- Data-driven decisions are made.
- Students may be screened for special education services.

Figure 1.1: The intervention tiers of RTI.

Bender and Shores continue,

This model presents the basic concept of multitier instruction, in that most needs for most students are successful addressed in Tier One, whereas Tier Two interventions can alleviate learning problems for most students struggling in basic skills. Tier Three is, in most states, reserved for students with significant remediation needs, and in many cases, students in Tier Three interventions may have already been declared eligible for services for learning disabilities. (p. 4)

In Tier 1, all students receive high-quality instruction and behavioral and social-emotional supports. This is also referred to as universal instruction or core instruction. Ongoing assessments determine student progress and guide decisions about the effectiveness of instruction at this level. When students struggle, general education teachers may offer instructional supports such as reteaching, using graphic organizers, peer teaching, or other instructional practices considered to be effective practices for the specific learning need. Teachers assess to make sure the students are learning and send those who need supplemental instruction to Tier 2, where they will receive targeted interventions based on research. These interventions usually are provided at a specific time in the school schedule to small groups of students. According to IDEA Partnership (2007c), students served at Tier 2 are those whose performance on selected evaluation instruments shows that they are significantly behind in terms of performance and/or rate of progress on a given learning skill. IDEA emphasizes that "supplementary focused instruction does not mean the same strategies used for longer periods of time (more of the same) but different strategies with more intensity (frequency and duration)" (p. 16).

Additional data are collected on the effectiveness of the interventions, based on the progress of the students. Only after interventions at Tier 1 and Tier 2 have proven to be ineffective are students moved to Tier 3 for more specialized assessments and possible special education placement.

Thus, the steps to implementation in RTI are as follows:

1. Schoolwide screening measures are implemented for all students two to three times yearly.

2. Teams of educators review the screening data to determine student needs.

3. The three-tier system is employed to guide educators as they provide appropriate interventions. (Maanum, 2009)

Tier 1

In Tier 1, all students are screened to determine whether they are as proficient as expected for their age or grade level so that teachers can differentiate instruction for them as needed, instead of waiting for a student to fail. Data from Tier 1 will include assessments, interventions on identified skills, teacher observations, and other information. As Maanum (2009) describes it, the first supports for any learning gaps shown in these data occur in the general education classroom, in a large group or more general format, and are delivered by the regular classroom teacher. Usually, reteaching or scaffolding the learning to close gaps will be the only support necessary. It is estimated that 80 percent of the students in a classroom will not need interventions beyond this day-to-day reteaching and working with groups of students to help them reframe the learning in a way that matches their learning styles or fills in gaps from previous learning.

The assumption is that at Tier 1, all students will receive scientifically based instruction that has been proven to be effective, usually with effect sizes established by research. For example, IDEA 2004 specifies best practices as necessary to teach five elements of reading (300.309[a][1]):

1. Phonemic awareness
2. Phonics (sounds to letters)
3. Vocabulary
4. Reading fluency
5. Reading comprehension

Similarly, IDEA 2004 specifies four elements of mathematics most often targeted through effective instruction (300.309[a][1]):

1. Problem solving
2. Fluency
3. Conceptual knowledge
4. Communication/reasoning (Fletcher et al., n.d.)

Data related to adequate yearly progress (AYP) assessment of skills specified in state and local academic standards as well as individualized school data should guide the use of research-based instruction in the general education classroom setting at Tier 1.

Table 1.1 outlines the key elements of Tier 1.

Table 1.1: Tier 1 Overview

Students served	All students
Curriculum utilized	A scientific research-based curriculum with instructional strategies that make the most difference in student learning, modified for poverty and culture
Instructional time	Academic instructional time as set by the school district
Grouping	Large and small groups as needed
Persons responsible	Classroom teacher
Assessment	Universal screening of all students, usually at the beginning, middle, and end of the academic year, or more often
Location	General education classroom
Major difference in treatment	General instruction differentiated for student needs

Tier 2

Tier 2 provides additional instruction and assessment. As noted earlier, approximately 15 percent of the students in a typical classroom will need additional Tier 2 interventions in small-group settings for at least 30 minutes per day or the equivalent for eight to twelve weeks. These interventions are typically delivered by the regular classroom teacher and/or others designated for this task, such as a reading specialist or other support staff. Progress is monitored weekly.

The 15 percent of students who move to Tier 2 will need both continued core instruction (Tier 1) *and* targeted Tier 2 instruction in small groups for a period of time. The interventions at this level are more intense and focused than those provided in Tier 1; usually students work together on target skills in groups of two to four. Teachers keep individualized notes and reports on these students, tracking students' progress on the identified skills. Explicit rules exist for determining whether a learner is making progress. The IDEA Partnership (2007a) makes this point clear by stating that once an intervention is in place, the effectiveness of the intervention must be monitored before determining if the student should continue with the intervention, gradually be removed from the intervention (called "fading"), or be provided a new intervention.

Again, research-based interventions are an integral part of the process. IDEA makes the following recommendations at this level:

1. Interventions can be in a variety of settings or times of day. (extended day, tutorials, in-class)

2. As an intervention proves to be effective with a student it can be faded for that individual. However, it is important that guidelines are in place to help make informed data decisions about when to fade an intervention, to change it or to continue it.

3. In order for Tier Two to be effective, the interventions must be implemented appropriately, with intensity and fidelity.

4. Focused continuous progress monitoring of responsiveness to academic and/or behavioral interventions is critical to the process. (IDEA Partnership, 2007b, p. 20)

Again, without examining comprehensive information, teachers cannot ascertain whether students are not making progress because of ineffective instruction or inappropriate interventions modified for the effects of culture and poverty. This topic will be further discussed in the next chapter.

If students make progress and no longer need the intervention services, then they are removed from the intervention program. For students who continue to struggle or are deemed still to need the intervention, additional services may be provided. Specialized testing may be required to determine whether students need the services of Tier 3.

Table 1.2 outlines the key elements of Tier 2.

Table 1.2: Tier 2 Overview

Students served	Students who did not respond to Tier 1 instruction
Curriculum utilized	A specialized scientific research-based intervention that has a high effect size on student learning, modified for poverty and culture as appropriate
Instructional time	Academic core instructional time as set by the school district with an additional time (perhaps 20–30 minutes) for interventions
Grouping	Small groups
Persons responsible	Classroom teacher and/or designated teacher, paraprofessional, or specialist
Assessment	Progress monitoring at least weekly on the targeted skills, looking for adequate progress over time
Location	General education classroom
Major difference in treatment	Small group and more intense than Tier 1

Tier 3

Finally, it is estimated that only 5 percent of a typical classroom will require more intense interventions at Tier 3. These interventions usually are specific in terms of the identified skills not mastered by the student, and specialized instruction usually is provided to individuals or pairs of students at designated times. Progress monitoring is individualized and occurs weekly.

Table 1.3 outlines the key elements of Tier 3.

Table 1.3: Tier 3 Overview

Students served	Students who have not responded adequately to Tier 1 and Tier 2 interventions
Curriculum utilized	Individualized and based on scientifically proven instruction
Instructional time	Academic core instructional time as set by the school district, with the addition of time for intensive intervention strategies
Grouping	Individual or small homogeneous groups
Persons responsible	Determined by the school district; may be the classroom teacher or specialized teachers or paraprofessionals
Assessment	Progress monitoring conducted at least weekly to determine if adequate progress is being made
Location	General education classroom or classroom designated by the school
Major difference in methods	Individualized intervention that is more intense than those used in Tiers 1 and 2

Tier 3 usually includes a comprehensive evaluation to determine whether the student needs the services of special education or other interventions. In the RTI model, students are not evaluated specifically as learning disabled until they get to Tier 3, and sometimes not until after Tier 3. The idea is that by providing early interventions and monitoring those interventions, fewer students will be mislabeled as learning disabled and those students who truly need special education services will be served.

Even when students are served at the Tier 3 level, the legislation makes clear that such students should be served in the general education classroom with specified modifications after careful review of data. RTI was designed to help ensure that students could be served in the general education classroom with the instructional modifications most appropriate for them.

The Role of Special Education in RTI

The goals of RTI are to prevent academic problems by responding early and to determine which students need to be served as learning disabled. It is the accuracy of the identification of a child as learning disabled that has created much of the dialogue about the changes in special education law. Much of the literature in the field suggests that many of those identified may be instructionally, rather than cognitively, disabled. Those instructional gaps may be the result of poor curriculum, lack of access to highly qualified teachers, lack of vocabulary skills, and myriad other problems over which the student has no control. We will explore this topic more in chapter 2.

What Is the Meaning of Learning Disabled?

If educators are going to get interventions and, more importantly, diagnoses correct, then they must look closely at the definition of *learning disabled* (LD) and how it has evolved from early legislation through the legislation that defines RTI. These questions—who are the children who need our help, how much help do they need, and how will we identify them?—lie at the heart of the problem of closing achievement gaps.

The statutory definition of what constitutes a learning disability first appeared in 1968 in a report from the National Advisory Committee on Handicapped Children:

> The term *specific learning disability* means a disorder in one or more of the basic psychological processes involved in understanding or in using language, spoken or written, which may manifest itself in an imperfect ability to listen, speak, read, write, spell, or to do mathematical calculations. (U.S. Office of Education, 1968)

This vague language led to varied interpretations. Different states (and even school districts within the same state) often used different formulas to diagnose LD, resulting in a lack of uniformity in identifying children for special education support. In 1977, the U.S. Department of Education Office of Special Education and Rehabilitation Services tried to clarify the definition by adding criteria that required a significant difference in IQ and achievement by the student. The change read, "a severe discrepancy between achievement and intellectual ability in one or more of the areas: (1) oral expression; (2) listening comprehension; (3) written expression; (4) basic reading skill; (5) reading comprehension; (6) mathematics calculation; or (7) mathematic reasoning" (United States Office of Education, 1977, p. G1082, as cited in Fletcher et al., n.d.).

Though the 1977 law encouraged multiple measures, it was often interpreted to mean that the single inclusionary criterion of IQ discrepancy was paramount. Thus schools sought tests that would determine any discrepancy between a student's IQ and his or her achievement in the classroom.

Federal regulations (IDEA 2004, 300.309[a][1]) now say that to qualify a child for special education services, the school must show that the child does not achieve adequately for the child's age or meet state-approved grade-level standards in one or more of the following:

1. Oral expression
2. Listening comprehension
3. Written expression
4. Basic reading skill
5. Reading fluency skills
6. Reading comprehension
7. Mathematics calculation
8. Mathematics problem solving

Under RTI, special education is seen as a separate entity, but all students are evaluated, and all students who need assistance— whether at the universal level (Tier 1) or at the more intense levels (Tiers 2 and 3)—are provided with targeted interventions. Assessment begins early and includes every child. Assessment does not wait for children to fail before triggering interventions. Progress monitoring is done not just once a year but continually, using various formats that are targeted to instructional goals.

Teachers use the research on duration, frequency, and time of interventions before moving to another step of their school model. Students are identified and assessed at two or more tiers. This means that students go through at least two increasingly intense levels of interventions and assessments prior to being considered for special education programs. Response to intervention authority Jim Wright (2006) reports the process succinctly:

- A student with academic delays is given one or more research-validated interventions.

- The student's academic progress is monitored frequently to see if those interventions are sufficient to help the student to catch up with his or her peers.

- If the student fails to show significantly improved academic skills despite several well-designed and implemented interventions, this failure to "respond to intervention" can be viewed as evidence of an underlying Learning Disability.

This is the most significant change from the discrepancy model used prior to RTI. According to IDEA 2004, § 300.307 on specific learning disabilities:

(a) *General.* A State must adopt . . . criteria for determining whether a child has a specific learning disability. . . . The criteria adopted by the State—

(1) Must not require the use of severe discrepancy between intellectual ability and achievement for determining whether a child has a specific learning disability, as defined in § 300.8(c)(10);

(2) Must permit the use of a process based on the child's response to scientific, research-based intervention

IDEA 2004 provides an additional inclusionary criterion that must be assessed regardless of the identification model employed:

To ensure that underachievement in a child suspected of having a specific learning disability is not due to lack of appropriate instruction in reading or math, the group must consider, as part of the evaluation . . . (1) Data that

> demonstrate that prior to, or as a part of, the referral process, the child was provided appropriate instruction in regular education settings, delivered by qualified personnel; and (2) Data-based documentation of repeated assessments of achievement at reasonable intervals, reflecting formal assessment of student progress during instruction, which was provided to the child's parents. (IDEA 2004, § 300.309[a][1])

Thus, it is no longer acceptable to determine that a child is learning disabled simply by showing that a child has struggled or indeed has failed in school. Instead, schools must document that the *school* has already done all that is possible, through research-based instruction and intervention, to alleviate the child's learning gap, leaving a specific learning disability as the only remaining possible reason for the learning gap.

Why Did the Discrepancy Model Fail?

Under the discrepancy model, students with academic delays (observed and/or tested) would be given a battery of tests that included an IQ test and an achievement test. At that time we believed that an IQ test would give us a picture of what the child was capable of learning, while the achievement test would give us data on what the student had learned. If there was a significant gap between the IQ score and the achievement score, a formula was used to determine whether the gap was severe. If the gap between achievement and IQ was determined by a prescribed formula to be severe, the student would be diagnosed with a learning disability. Some of the problems with the discrepancy model, as identified by Gresham (2001) and quoted by Wright (2006), are:

- "[It] requires chronic school failure BEFORE remedial/ special education supports can be given.

- [It] fails to consider that outside factors such as poor or inconsistent instruction may contribute to a child's learning delay.

- A 'severe discrepancy' between test scores provides no useful information about WHY the student is doing poorly academically."

According to Fletcher (n.d.), this approach to identification was predominant for the next thirty years, despite warnings and protests from the field: "The construct of LD became aligned with IQ-discrepancy to a point where contrary evidence and major measurement issues were not given serious consideration."

What kinds of contrary evidence? Alarm bells were being sounded about the disproportionate number of minority and poor students being classified as LD. Some students simply did not speak English as a first language or lacked the vocabulary of their classmates; teachers know that students from poverty often come to school with half the vocabulary of students who are not in poverty (Marzano & Kendall, 1996). Many of these students continue to be mistakenly placed in special education for learning disabilities when, in fact, they do not have trouble learning but simply have not been exposed to the vocabulary of the middle-class classroom. The President's Commission on Excellence in Special Education (2002) stated that in the absence of RTI evidence, many students placed in special education are "instructional casualties."

In the *RTI and SLD Identification Presenter's Guide*, the IDEA Partnership (2007c), a collaborative partnership of many professional and family organizations, cites these problems with previous methods of special needs identification:

- **A long wait for help**— Prior to the amendments to IDEA in 2004, a child had to demonstrate a discrepancy between general intellectual functioning (IQ) and academic achievement before qualifying for special education services. A child had to be engaged in formal education long enough for achievement tests to be accurate and to reveal a discrepancy between the results and the child's IQ. Thus, in what was called the wait-to-fail model, a child often had to fail repeatedly before an intervention was offered. Under the amendments to IDEA in 2004, interventions take place as soon as possible, without regard to discrepancy between IQ and achievement, in order to avoid failure altogether.

■ **Misidentification**—Not all students who need intervention need special education. Students who do not receive interventions in the general education classroom for learning difficulties due to not understanding or not receiving differentiated instruction may experience failure and be inaccurately identified as specific learning disabled (SLD). According to the IDEA Partnership (2007c), "50% of students with Individual Education Plans are identified as SLD. 80–90% of these currently identified as children with SLD are identified because of reading difficulties" (p. 33).

■ **Disproportionate representation**—If we look at the numbers of students in certain groups—such as African American, Hispanic, and Native American/Alaska Native—and then look at the numbers in special education, we will find that there is a disproportionate number in special education. In addition, we will find that there are discrepancies in terms of gender:

   ▪ There are twice as many males as females in special education in the primary school.

   ▪ 75 percent of students with SLD are male.

   ▪ 76 percent of students with emotional disabilities (ED) are male.

   ▪ More than 50 percent of students with communication disorders (CD) are male. (IDEA Partnership, 2007c)

Over the years, LD often has become a catchall for students who are not performing according to the expectations of the classroom teacher. This could mean anything from reading issues to behavioral problems. For example, if a child comes to kindergarten or first grade and does not appropriately respond to reading or speaking because he or she lacks vocabulary, it is no surprise if he or she is placed in a special education program.

Many of the students labeled as learning disabled have nothing neurologically or physically wrong with them. Simply put, LD students too often are those who do not fit the mold of the typical North American school.

What's So Bad About Special Education?

The question arises, what is wrong with that? Some might suggest that even if these students are not really learning disabled, at least they are being served in special education. That would not be so bad if such placement ensured that their needs were met—if students lacking vocabulary, for example, received immersion in vocabulary. But because of the special education label, they are not likely to receive that intervention.

In fact, data show that students placed in special education rarely return to general education. Less than 10 percent of special education students return to and stay in mainstream classrooms (Kunjufu, 2005). Additionally, only 27 percent of African American males in special education graduate from high school. Eighty percent of the students in special education are deficient in reading and writing; in fact the prison system projects its new construction on current fourth-grade reading scores (Kunjufu, 2005). If these statistics do not make educators and policymakers think carefully about the difference that special education placement and effective education make in students' lives, then perhaps a look at the costs of miseducation will. In 2005, the cost of educating a child in the general education program averaged $7,000 per student, while the cost to educate a student in special education averaged $12,000 (Kunjufu, 2005). Historically, the federal government has only picked up about 20 percent of the cost of special education services.

The concept of *services* merits emphasis because special education seeks to provide services beyond those of the regular curriculum for students who are not successful in general education. One way to understand what is a learning disability is to consider what it is not. Learning disabled services are not designed for students who are unsuccessful in school simply because of:

- Inadequate preschool experiences

- Inadequate educational opportunities

- Inadequate language skills

- Learning gaps as a result of the home or the education system

- Cultural differences in the way students learn

Age-appropriateness also is a factor in determining whether a child should be considered for LD placement. Age-appropriateness is based on grade-level standards. An example might be the standards for listening and comprehension. McREL, a respected research group, provides reliable information for reviewing individual states' standards. Following, for instance, are characteristics typical for a K–2 student in reading comprehension:

1. Uses mental images based on pictures and print to aid comprehension

2. Uses meaning clues (e.g., picture captions, title, cover, headings, story structure, story topic) to aid comprehension and make predictions about content (e.g., action, events, character's behavior (McREL, 2010)

From this information, a first-grade teacher knows what to expect from his or her students. After directly teaching students how to use elements such as picture captions, title, cover, and so on, the teacher can assess whether students use these items to help them understand a story and make reasonable content predictions. Effective instructional strategies might include showing students exactly where such elements can be found in their books or sending them on a scavenger hunt in their books to find the information about stories they will read. Students also will need vocabulary words, such as *caption, title, cover, headings, story strategy,* and so forth. Teachers should not assume that students already know these terms or even that they have ready access to books.

In theory, RTI is a wonderful gift to all students because it holds the promise that not only will students no longer "fall through the cracks," they will also not be incorrectly placed into special programs. I say "in theory" because until we provide educators with the necessary tools to evaluate and determine which instructional skills make the most difference in student learning, interventions will not be effective. The tenets of response to intervention are a guide, a process to be applied to a school's plan. RTI becomes functional only when the tenets are placed into an in-depth written plan that is used to guide decisions.

In Conclusion

Most classroom teachers do everything they know how to do to help students succeed. Often, however, administration has neither delivered pertinent research results on effective teaching to teachers nor provided appropriate staff development on how to implement that research. This chapter has examined RTI legal history and its relationship to special education, the structure of the three-tier RTI model, and the promises that each tier's principles and applications hold for students.

Learning Log

In this chapter	Your thoughts
In this chapter, we discussed the fundamentals of the RTI program. What policies are already in place at your school that will help you make decisions about appropriate interventions?	
In the next chapter	
In the next chapter, we will examine the impact of poverty and culture on student learning and on identification of their needs. What do you believe about how poverty and culture impact student learning? In what ways does your school address those factors?	

Chapter two
Understanding the Impact of Poverty and Culture

Volumes have been written about closing gaps in achievement, and millions of dollars have been spent trying to find ways to help all students be successful—yet achievement gaps persist for some groups of students. Many schools have implemented their own interpretations of response to intervention in an effort to close those gaps, but even if undertaken with the best intentions, these interpretations will not make the expected difference unless they address two hidden issues: poverty and culture. If RTI is to fulfill its promise—if educators are truly going to assess learning difficulties versus instructional mistakes, and then address those difficulties successfully—then we must direct more attention toward alleviating the effects of poverty and culture.

Do Minority and Poor Children Really Have Equal Access?

The Supreme Court ruled that separate is not equal. And yet, because in many urban areas the more affluent have moved to suburbs, cities often have been left with segregated schools through attrition. Many urban facilities are older and lack the wiring capacity for newer technology. They often have younger, less-experienced staff and may lack the materials and equipment for high-quality learning.

Carmen Arroyo (2008), writing for the Education Trust, says that although society likes to *say* to all students that getting a good education is one of the most important things they can do, we put students at the mercy of their states, provinces, regions, and school districts when it comes to actually getting an education and where that education will take place. She goes on to say:

> Unfortunately, too many states provide no such assurance [of a good education] for students who need it most. Despite national imagery full of high-flying concepts like "equal opportunity" and "level playing field," English-learner, low-income and minority students do not get the extra school supports they need to catch up to their more advantaged peers; they all too frequently receive less than do other students. (p. 1)

The Education Trust (2008) collected data from Texas schools to prove this point. It should be noted that although their report, *Their Fair Share: How Texas-Sized Gaps in Teacher Quality Shortchange Poor and Minority Students*, cited many states for unequal opportunities, data were collected for only one of those states, Texas. The report noted gaps in opportunities for students in the following areas:

- **Teacher quality**—The report found that Hispanic, African American, and low-income students are "less likely to be assigned to teachers who are fully credentialed; less likely to be in classrooms with experienced teachers; and less likely to attend schools with a stable teaching force" (Education Trust, 2008, p. 6).

- **Teacher experience**—According to the report, "Hispanic and African American and low-income students in Texas's 50 largest districts are less likely than their white and affluent peers to be in classrooms with experienced teachers" (p. 14). No one would argue with the fact that new teachers sometimes are stronger in new pedagogy than their experienced counterparts, but data prove that experience matters. According to a report by Clotfelter, Ladd, and Vigdor (2007), a teacher with three to five years of experience has four to seven times the effect on students' math achievement than does reducing class size by five students.

- **Stability**—According to Ed Fuller of the University of Texas (Education Trust, 2008), teachers, on average, make almost a thousand dollars less than comparable colleagues each year if they teach in high-poverty or high-minority areas. The report found that for most of the largest school districts studied, students who were minority or low income were likely to attend schools where high numbers of teachers were leaving the field or transferring to other schools each year. The authors of the report noted, "We often talk a lot about damage done by the lack of stability in low-income and minority students' home lives, but we rarely examine the effect of instability in their *school* lives" (Education Trust, 2008, p. 20, emphasis added).

All of the research presented here would lead to the conclusion that when it comes to closing gaps in achievement, the teacher matters most. Yet schools more often than not assign students with the most needs to the least-qualified teachers.

Fidelity and the Funding Gap

If all children are to be taught by highly qualified teachers using a curriculum that is high quality and standards based, and if they are to be taught with research-based instructional techniques that are considered to be best practices, then the results should be higher levels of student learning. For this to happen, however, schools must make improvements in how students are assessed and taught. Some schools will need to take giant leaps forward to help their students achieve.

In 2005, the Education Trust released a startling report called *The Funding Gap*, which revealed that many American children enter school each year already behind their age peers in basic knowledge. While this finding was not a surprise to anyone in education, what followed might have surprised many readers:

> What [Americans] don't know, however, is that instead of organizing our educational systems to make things better for these children, we organize our systems of public education in ways that make things worse. One way we do that is by simply spending less in schools serving high concentrations of low income and minority children than we do on schools serving more affluent and white children. (Education Trust, 2005, p. 1)

The report went on to say that, on average, the United States spends $900 a year less per student on educating students in schools with the most children from poverty than it spends in schools serving more affluent students. In a study of the 2004–2005 school year, the Education Trust looked at the spending levels between high- and low-poverty districts in forty-eight states. The report is very telling in terms of spending on high-priority students. Only eighteen states spent more per student in high-poverty districts. Sixteen actually spent *less* per student in high-poverty districts, while fifteen spent the same amount in both high- and low-poverty districts (Education Trust, 2005).

For response to intervention, this means that schools in high-poverty areas need high-quality staff and materials just to begin RTI on the same footing as other schools. Money alone does not solve problems, but money wisely spent to provide high-quality teachers who stay abreast of research-based instructional methods and have the materials to provide an enriched curriculum does make a difference.

What Is Poverty?

Poverty is viewed in various ways. When some people think of poverty, they may conjure up images of starving children in undeveloped countries rather than scenes from North America. Ruby Payne (2001) views poverty in terms of deficits, such as lack of emotional support, lack of goods, lack of nourishment, and so on. For most educators, poverty is defined by the U.S. Census Bureau, which publishes a level-of-income chart adjusted for the number of people living in the household. This information also provides guidelines used by most schools in determining which students are eligible for free or reduced-price lunches. It also forms the guidelines used most often for Title I funding. Unfortunately, there are discrepancies in the information, because the figures assume that the financial burdens of, for instance, a five-member family in New York City are the same as those for a similar-size family in Iowa City. If researchers truly examined costs of living by city and state, the number of individuals and families living in poverty probably would be even larger than the 40 million–plus now reported.

Although white children represent the largest number of all children living in poverty in the United States, other racial groups have comparatively larger *percentages* of children living in poverty. According to Kunjufu (2005):

> From an aggregate perspective, there are more whites below the poverty line than African Americans—20 million to 9 million. From a percentage perspective, 25 percent of African Americans live below the poverty line and only 10 percent of whites. (p. 29)

Kunjufu also points out that African Americans in poverty live mainly in densely populated urban areas, while poor whites more often are scattered in rural areas and mountain regions, living in mobile homes and other types of substandard housing.

The Impact of Poverty on Student Learning

According to a study by Wenglinsky (2002) from the Education Policy Analysis Archives, the effect size of poverty on student learning is .76, which translates into an effect on achievement of 28 percentile points. In other words, if the average student in poverty is achieving at the 50th percentile and the teacher has a magic wand that can take away the effects of poverty on learning, then the teacher could move that child to the 78th percentile.

While that is significant, there is more to learn. Wenglinsky (2002) suggests that when educators know and correctly use effective instructional practices, teachers achieve an effect size of .98 and can move that poverty-influenced average 34 percentile points. Thus, a teacher can move the class average to the 84th percentile without magic—just effective instruction.

Why Are More Minority and Poor Children in Special Education?

Knowing that effective instruction is more powerful than income level in affecting student achievement may cause us to question some of our assumptions about the origins of the achievement gap. If we have the power to overcome economic disadvantages in the classroom, why don't we? What other "disadvantages" are perpetuated through the educational system? In fact, response to intervention became a formal part of the 2004 reauthorization of the Individuals with Disabilities Education Act partially as an effort to reduce the growing number of students incorrectly assigned to the learning disability category, in particular the disproportionate numbers of minority and economically disadvantaged students receiving special education services under this label. According to Hosp (2009):

> The basic premise of disproportionate representation is that, all other things being similar, students from different groups should be identified for special education services in similar proportions. For example, if 6% of the Caucasian students in a given district are identified for special education, we would expect about 6% of the African-American students, 6% of the Latino/a students and 6% of any other group identified. (p. 1)

The same can be said if a group is underrepresented. This measure is used not only when examining data on ethnicity, but also when looking at other measures, such as language proficiency, gender, culture, and so on.

IDEA 2004 describes how school RTI programs can commit funds to address the specific problems of over-representation:

An LEA may use up to 15% of its IDEA Part B funds in any fiscal year, less any funds reduced from its local fiscal effort, to develop and implement coordinated, early intervening services. Coordinated early intervening services may include interagency financing structures (for students in K–12 with a particular emphasis on students in K–3) who have not been identified as needing special education or related services but who need additional academic and behavioral support to succeed in a general education environment. When it has been determined that there is significant disproportionality with respect to the identification of children as children with disabilities, or the placement in particular educational settings of such children, the SEA shall require the LEA to reserve the maximum 15% of IDEA Part B funds to provide comprehensive coordinated early intervention services to serve children in the LEA, particularly children in those groups that were significantly over-identified. (as cited by National Center for Learning Disabilities, 2010)

That is, IDEA 2004 clearly states that funds for early intervening services can be used not just for children in special education, but for any struggling child—particularly children from groups over represented in special education. A major change made in the 2004 IDEA legislation is its focus on inclusionary criteria. IDEA 2004 "requires consideration of factors that might indicate that low achievement is due to factors that do not represent LD" (Fletcher, n.d.). IDEA was never intended to be a justification for dumping children who learn or behave in ways that are different from most students into special education classes. But the problem of misidentification persists.

According to Hosp (2009), the U.S. Department of Education Office of Civil Rights (OCR) began conducting a biennial survey of elementary and secondary schools in the United States as early as 1968 and continues to do so today (see Donovan & Cross, 2002, for a more detailed description). One focus of the data in these surveys has been placement of students into special education programs disaggregated by various student characteristics (for example, gender, race, ethnicity, receipt of free or reduced-price lunch, or language proficiency). As noted in the previous chapter, African American males make up 8 percent of the population of public schools, and yet they make up 30 percent of students placed in special education (Kunjufu, 2005). As a matter of fact, African American males are placed in special education more than any other single group. The group least likely to be placed in special education is white females. Patterns of disproportionality, especially in SLD, have continued to increase at the national level for the past forty years. These patterns reveal more about us as educators than our students; they tell us not that students of various subgroups deserve to be in special education, but that we are predisposed to put them there.

Kunjufu also points out the disproportionate percentage of African American students, particularly males, who are labeled as ADD (attention deficit disorder), ADHD (attention deficit hyperactive disorder), EMR (educable mentally retarded), and LD (learning disabled). We know that there are some basic behavioral differences in males and females (exceptions exist, of course). According to Kunjufu (2005), boys tend to:

- Be more aggressive
- Have a higher energy level
- Have a shorter attention span
- Have a slower maturation rate
- Be less cooperative
- Be physically larger
- Be influenced more by peer group
- Like math over reading
- Have gross motor skills that are more developed than fine motor skills
- Be less neat than girls
- Be louder
- Have a distinctive walk
- Have a larger or more sensitive ego
- Have hearing that is inferior to girls (primary school) (Kunjufu, 2005, p. 88)

If we know these things, he asks, what changes have we made to account for and deal with the differences?

We also must question the correlation of health issues such as poor nutrition and exposure to lead with the number of impoverished minority students in special education. For instance, how do schools account for the fact that 30 percent of the African American male student population is in special education but only 10 percent (Kunjufu, 2005) of the African American female student population? If the health issue premise were true for minority students generally, would not both males and females equally be affected?

Since placement for ADD and ADHD represents 50 percent of the diagnoses for all students placed in special education, these are particularly important subcategories to examine if educators are going to get placement right (Kunjufu, 2005). The *Diagnostic and Statistical Manual of Mental Disorders* (*DSM-IV-TR*) defines hyperactivity in this way:

> Six or more of the following symptoms of hyperactivity-impulsivity have persisted for at least six months to a degree that it is maladaptive and inconsistent with developmental level.
>
> **Hyperactivity**
>
> a. Often fidgets with hands or feet or squirms in seat
>
> b. Often leaves seat in classroom or other situations in which remaining seated is expected
>
> c. Often runs about or climbs excessively in situations in which it is inappropriate [. . .]
>
> d. Often has difficulty playing or engaging in leisure activities quietly
>
> e. Is often "on the go" or often acts as if "driven by a motor"
>
> f. Often talks excessively
>
> **Impulsivity**
>
> a. Often blurts out answers before questions have been completed

b. Often has difficulty awaiting turn

c. Often interrupts or intrudes on others (e.g., butts into conversations or games) (as cited by University of California, Berkeley, 2010)

This definition is highly subjective in that it calls for the educator to make a judgment based on observations and interpretations and to determine what counts as "often" or "excessive." Kunjufu (2005) suggests that the large number of African American students are placed in special education because they come from a culture of hands-on learning instead of one dominated by sitting and listening: "one of the major reasons for African American males being disproportionately placed in special education classes is because the regular classroom is not culturally sensitive to the needs of this unique population" (p. vii).

The RTI model gives hope that disproportionality will be addressed and eradicated. How can RTI help us to do this? Hosp (2009) says that RTI will help address the issue of disproportionality in three ways:

1. **Focus on outcomes**—Because RTI focuses on the achievement outcomes of all students, interventions will be evaluated according to their effectiveness rather than mere compliance.

2. **Focus on the individual**—In RTI, students are examined individually for learning gaps and provided with the most appropriate interventions for their individual needs, thus improving the odds of success.

3. **Focus on data**—Although we have always collected data on students, the collection has not always been universal or consistent. Often data were collected only on individual students who demonstrated failure over time, and thus the data could not be analyzed for trends by ethnicity, socioeconomic status, gender, and so on. The new focus on collecting data on all students means that group discrepancies and trends should show up quickly when we disaggregate and analyze the data for patterns.

The "Ideal" Student

Kunjufu (2005) questions how the ideal student in the minds of most teachers today relates to the average African American male student. The model that we use to determine the ideal, he suggests, may in fact be based on the white female student (as most teachers in the U.S. are white females). Some of the criteria that educators often describe as ideal include:

- Quiet
- Can sit for long periods of time
- A long attention span
- Can work independently
- Likes ditto sheets
- A left-brain learner
- Passive
- Cooperative
- Teacher pleaser
- Learned reading before the second grade
- Well developed fine motor skills
- Neat
- Good handwriting
- Well organized
- Speaks standard English
- Two-parent home
- Middle class (Kunjufu, 2005, p. 28)

Could these teacher preferences for certain learning styles and teacher expectations of prior knowledge contribute to the fact that 80 percent of the African American children placed in special education are black males? For that matter, could it contribute to the fact that there are twice as many males of all races in special education as there are females?

A Note on Behavior Issues

Although response to intervention legislation addresses behavior as well as academics, this book deals primarily with the issues involved in learning itself, rather than the issues of behavior. Granted, the issues of learning are directly involved in behavior. For example, if a class is studying symmetry and a student has no idea what the word *symmetry* means, he or she may exhibit problematic behavior out of boredom. As for academics, response to intervention deals with behavior issues by providing interventions before the behavior leads to failure or more advanced forms of behavior issues.

Sousa (2008) tells us that:

> behavior is the result of genetic and environmental (social) factors. The genes that now underlie the behavior differences between males and females must have been selected because they improved the chances that an individual of that gender would survive and reproduce. If we accept the theories about the different roles that our male and female ancestors played, then it becomes possible to understand why their behavior and associated cognitive skills developed differently. (p. 68)

There is not enough space in this book to deal with all of the issues involved, but here are some suggestions as you look at behavior:

1. Understand that the ideal behavior envisioned by teachers is often based on the model of an Anglo-Saxon female.

2. In some cultures, movement and talking to each other are regarded as good things. Provide opportunities for students to move, and use music where appropriate to help with the learning. Sousa (2008) says that movement is important for young males and suggests that teachers consider using music, rhymes, and movement to teach concepts.

3. The literature offered in the elementary classrooms may not have any relevance to males, especially those from a culture that expects boys to be "macho" from an early age. Often the literature available is very "white" in nature and

does not have much to do with the world of an African American, Native American, or Hispanic student. Choose materials that are relevant to students to keep their attention on the work.

4. The criteria used by many states to determine ADD and ADHD tendencies may be considered to be descriptive of some cultures in general.

5. Understand the gender-based differences in boys and girls. Males tend to be more boisterous in the classroom and may be identified as having a behavior problem. According to Sousa (2008), boys are more likely to participate in discussions in literature when the reading is about good and evil, heroes and villains, or right and wrong.

6. As Sousa (2008) explains:

   Students with social and emotional problems often have distorted and negative attitudes and stereotypes about their family, school, peers, or even themselves. These attitudes and stereotypes may indeed be in conflict with their core beliefs, but they have not had the opportunity to do the cognitive reflection necessary to recognize this conflict exists. Interventions therefore that help students reflect on their misbehavior and on the degree to which that misbehavior is directed by their attitudes and stereotypes are likely to be successful. (p. 16)

We have seen that effective instruction has a greater effect on student achievement than income level, and yet minority students even from higher-income families are still struggling, as the last chapter noted. We've seen that some children simply do not fit our ideas of what they "should" be to succeed academically. So when we asked why have we failed to close the gap, we can see that the answer lies in the culture of our classrooms and its hidden cultural preferences that put some students at a disadvantage for academic success. No one argues that poverty has negative effects related to such things as health care, emotional wellness, exposure to enriched experiences, and early literacy, but culture—of the classroom and of our students—affects the way students learn far more than poverty. Fortunately, while funding issues are perennial, every educator can learn how to understand and address the cultural issues that have contributed to the achievement gap.

What Is Culture?

According to the U.S. Department of Health and Human Services, the official definition of culture is "broadly defined as a common heritage or set of beliefs, norms and values. It refers to the shared and largely learned, attributes of a group of people" (2001, p. 9).

Simply put, culture is the lens through which individuals view the world. Culture sometimes is equated with race, but many cultures exist within any racial group. Think of a landscape that has changed over time through various weather patterns, winds, pollution, and effects brought about by humans, animals, insects, birds, fish, and so on. What the landscape has become as a result of all of those influences is its culture. The same is true with humans. From birth, we are influenced by our caregivers, by where we live, by religion, by education, by experiences bad and good, by language, by other people, and by the rules and value systems of our society. All of our cultural influences affect how we approach learning. It is easy to expect students in our classrooms to have the same worldview that we have, but their worldviews may be very different based on their past experiences. For example, Clauss-Ehlers (2006) reminds us that the Western culture that dominates today's classrooms values competition, yet many cultures value the ability to problem solve with others more highly than competition. We need to understand our students and their families in the context of their worldview, which dictates what is valued. Difficulties arise in the classroom when the teacher or other educators try to impose their set of beliefs on students who have come from a different cultural experience.

According to Norman Doidge (2007), our brain is wiring and rewiring itself throughout our lives, based on those things that gain our attention and time. The brain we are born with is not the brain we die with, he says. Humans come into the world with about half of their neurological wiring in place; survival instincts are hardwired, for example. The other half is largely determined by environment; our brain is constantly changing itself based on our environment, and we build dendrites all through our lives. Children who play video games for hours are rewiring their brains, as are those who are reading or watching television. The rewiring is just different based on the activity on which they focus. Researchers once thought that at a certain age humans quit producing dendrites and that simple "pruning" subsequently took place. Thanks to the study of neuroplasticity, we now understand that humans learn and produce dendrites throughout life and that the human brain is malleable—that is, it is capable of changing throughout life (Doidge, 2007).

The significance of this information to implementing RTI is that educators must be aware that they teach to many different cultures. Students' brain wiring has been influenced by their cultures, students in today's classrooms are different from the students of even five years ago, and not all students learn well in the typical North American school—but we can find ways to modify the typical North American school to meet their needs. We are all lifelong learners, whether we intend to be or not, and thus it is important that we help students find ways that they learn best. Through different interventions, we help students to learn beyond what might have been perceived as their limits. The healthy brain is limited only by its experiences.

Cultural Identity

Culture gives people a sense of identity. A person's own culture often is invisible to him because of its familiarity. Cultures outside one's own may seem like "others"; people sometimes say, "I don't know why 'they' do things that way." To understand culture, it is necessary to look at two aspects of identity. First, *ethnic identity* is the individual's membership in a social group with common characteristics, such as language, history, geography, and often physical characteristics (Fisherman, 1989; Sheets, 2008). For example, Hispanic culture may include people from Mexico and South America, despite geographical and political differences.

Second is *cultural identity*, which is broader in scope as it crosses ethnic groups. Researchers note, "Social groups existing within one nation may share a common language and a broad cultural identity but have distinct ethnic identities associated with a different language and history. Ethnic groups in the United States are examples of this" (Northeast and Islands Regional Educational Laboratory at Brown University, 2002, p. 4).

We sometimes think of culture in terms of race or ethnicity, but culture goes across racial and ethnic lines. An African American child who grows up in a rural area or who comes to us from another country is very different from the African American child who grows up in an urban area wrecked by violence and gangs.

In their book *Cultural Proficiency: A Manual for School Leaders*, Lindsey, Robins, and Terrell (2009), using the work of Ogbu (1992), discuss two types of ethnic minorities in the United States and Canada and their effects on learning. People with *immigrant status* have come to the United States or Canada voluntarily and tend to assimilate into the dominant culture. Individuals in this group usually leave behind much of their distinctive cultural membership as they blend into the majority population. They also tend to cross economic class boundaries in one or two generations. Immigrants are strongly affected by teaching and learning, the authors suggest, because they typically believe that education is crucial to becoming part of mainstream society. In the formation of the United States and Canada, immigrants from Europe brought what has become the dominant North American culture. Their beliefs and values created an environment in which education is viewed as the key to success.

People from *caste minorities*, on the other hand, were brought to or assimilated with the host country involuntarily and often have been kept in the lowest economic class by the dominant culture (Lindsey, Robins, & Terrell, 2009). Their perception is that education will not help them to become part of mainstream society. Many African Americans arrived as slaves and involuntarily joined the population; Native Americans were essentially exiled to small parcels of land. Latinos and Asians also have been segregated from the dominant society because of their languages. Lindsey, Robins, and Terrell (2009) put it succinctly: "Clearly, African American, First Nations, Mexican American, Puerto Rican, and Asian American feelings of alienation from the dominant society are not difficult to recognize and understand in this context of legally sanctioned segregation and exclusion" (p. 36). Educators must acknowledge these attitudes and their potential effect on students' experiences in the education system.

Classroom Culture

We must also acknowledge that classrooms and the education system in general also have a cultural identity. Typical North American schools are built around the Anglo-European model for middle- and upper-class students. Working independently is encouraged, sometimes demanded, because individual achievement is valued. Communication uses distal modes, such as reading and writing. In this culture, particularly in the age of standards and high-stakes testing, instruction focuses on delivering substance first, building relationships second. Schools in North America tend to emphasize competition for grades, achievement, and recognition. A pervasive belief has been that students should not share information—in many schools, doing so constitutes cheating.

Almost every other culture in the world, however, believes in collaborative learning and values the ability to share information and create relationships. Many cultures prize interdependence rather than individuality or solo achievement. Communication includes important proximal modes, such as touching and holding. From this perspective, in order for learning to take place, relationships must be forged first, then substance presented (Tileston & Darling, 2009). If educators do not recognize that students learn according to the norms of their culture and that those patterns of learning often are very different than the learning experiences offered in traditional North American schools, then we will perpetuate gaps in achievement.

Table 2.1 illustrates some of the differences between the individualist learning ethos of a typical North American school and the collectivist ethos found in many other cultures.

Table 2.1: Collectivist Versus Individualist Value Systems

Collectivist	Individualist
Native American Indians, Native Hawaiians, Native Alaskans, Latin Americans, Africans, Asians, Arabs	Anglo-Saxon and Northern European Americans
Emphasizes interdependence	Encourages independence
Preserves relationships, which are hierarchically structured around family roles and multiple generations	Values individual achievement
Defines intelligence as knowing how to successfully play one's role in the family or community	Views intelligence as competitive and aggressive
Regards the purpose of physical objects, like toys, as mediating social relationships; values them because they can be shared with someone else	Regards the purpose of physical objects, like toys, as developing skills in manipulating objects to become more competent and able to construct knowledge of the physical world
Communication includes proximal modes such as touching and holding.	Communication includes distal modes through linguistic means such as reading and writing.
Parents are more likely to promote their children's social intelligence and to emphasize interpersonal relationships, respect for elders and tradition, responsibility for others, and cooperation (relationship first; substance second).	Schools and parents define children's early cognitive development in terms of their knowledge of the physical world and linguistic communication skills (substance first, relationship second).

Sources: Barakat, 1993; Blake, 1994; Delgado Gaitan, 1993; Greenfield, Brazelton, & Childs, 1989; Hofstede, 1983; Kim & Choi, 1994; Lebra, 1994; Small, 1998; Suina & Smolkin, 1994; Tileston & Darling, 2009.

Individuals in most cultures learn within their own cultural context, which may not follow the linear, step-by-step methods of dominant-culture classrooms. According to Villegas (1991), Shade (1994), and Gay (2002), many African American children prefer oral presentations, social interactions, and tactile information. When acquiring information, they learn best through visual media, such as pictures, photographs, symbols, and multisensory approaches (including movement images, verbal communication, and sound). Most classrooms, however, are dominated by passive, single-modal approaches.

Similarly, children who learn best in the context of a story may have difficulty in a classroom where the answers to questions are expected to be provided in a linear fashion. If a teacher introduces a lesson on Johnny Appleseed to these students, he or she might first ask them if they know the parts of an apple. A child of Mexican heritage might answer with a story such as, "My grandmother and I make apple empanadas together. We wash the apples and then take out the stems. Next, we take off the peel. . . ." If teachers do not understand the child's cultural tendency to communicate in story, then they may think that student does not know the parts of an apple or that the student is simply wasting time.

The Impact of Culture on Student Learning

For students who learn easily and who adapt well to the style of the teacher, cultural learning preferences may not be a problem—except for boredom. For students who are struggling, however, teaching to their dominant modalities is critical. According to Jensen (2003), many of these students will never learn until they are taught in the modality most comfortable for them. Giving students more of the same, if the same is not working, is not a good intervention. If teachers are not provided training in working with diverse cultural groups, then some of the same instructional mistakes are likely to occur under the RTI model as happens under IQ-discrepancy models that have failed children from poverty and nondominant cultures. Remember, according to Marzano and Kendall (1996), students from poverty tend to start school with one-half the middle-class vocabulary necessary for success in school. Add to that the fact that 85 percent of any state's high-stakes test is based on vocabulary (Marzano & Kendall, 1996), and you have a double whammy on the success of minority and poor children. If a child who is of minority race and who is poor enters a class-room based on the principles of a European and Anglo-Saxon heritage, and if that child has one-half the vocabulary of the other children, what is bound to happen? Unless the school is knowledgeable in terms of progressive research, that child will go quickly to special education and will stay there—when all that may be needed is strong vocabulary instruction.

Educators must differentiate the instruction to maximize the child's learning strengths. If they take into account the culture and language acquisition skills of learners, educators may be less likely to make culturally biased judgments of learners' abilities— less likely, for example, to identify a child from inner-city poverty, a culture in which hands-on learning and movement are critical, as being hyperactive. As noted earlier, it costs on average $7,000 a year to educate a child in a general education classroom com-pared to $12,000 in a special education setting (Kunjufu, 2005). What if that money was spent, instead, on determining how best to teach students who do not learn in traditional ways? What if all teachers were trained to provide differentiated instruction that would better meet the educational needs of students from poverty backgrounds and various cultural heritages? It *can* be done—and it can be done in a way that raises the learning level for all children (Tileston & Darling, 2009).

In Conclusion

This chapter has explored some of the inequities that exist in schools today and has explained why, if left unaddressed, such inequities perpetuate achievement gaps. Poor and minority stu-dents do not have access to the teacher quality of their advan-taged peers, and they do not always arrive at school with the prior knowledge their teachers expect or the cultural background upon which the school system is built. Because some students learn differently from the traditional methods of typical schools, they are set up to be incorrectly labeled as learning disabled.

These gaps can be and must be closed in the early stages of RTI development for schools. Otherwise, educators are likely to get the same results from RTI that they have attained in the past from other well-meaning but ineffective programs. The definitions of both poverty and culture are important for understanding why these factors make a difference in student learning and why their role is critical in appropriately identifying students for intervention and for designing the intervention itself.

The following chapters will show how to counteract the influences of poverty and culture through RTI implementation, as well as the specific modifications that will make a difference in the achievement of students from poverty or nondominant cultural backgrounds.

Learning Log

In this chapter	Your thoughts
In this chapter, we learned the importance of including modifications for culture and poverty. What kinds of cultural differences exist in your school or classroom? How do you help students from other cultures succeed within the school's culture?	
In the next chapter	
In the next chapter, we will examine the planning phase of RTI implementation. Are specific interventions in place in your school to ensure that cultural differences will be taken into account in the RTI program?	

Chapter three
Planning for RTI Implementation

As chapter 1 showed, both RTI and NCLB require that all students are guaranteed a high-quality education with highly qualified teachers and a curriculum that is rooted in scientific, research-based methods. The premise behind these promises is that students succeed in school because of the strength of the educational system. We know, however, that we will still have many students, especially in poor areas, who will not have certified teachers or teachers who know best instructional practices. Add to that the changing demographics of schools and the fact that so many teachers have not been trained on how to understand the impact of poverty and culture, much less how to modify instructional strategies for those factors, and we have a system that is still not ready to meet student needs.

Although RTI is a major step in ensuring that all children learn to high standards, it will be only as good as the planning and research that go into developing individual school plans. If a school's intervention process does not follow the basic principles of RTI—if the school does not have highly qualified teachers who know and use best practices—and if teachers do not modify instruction to address issues related to culture and poverty, then the school cannot expect to change anything by implementing RTI. Therefore, the most important step in creating and implementing RTI is planning. This chapter will explore forming the exploration and implementation team, the two planning phases, and pitfalls to be aware of in planning.

Forming the Team

Planning for implementation should be a coordinated team effort. Usually the team put together by the school or district is fairly small at this point in the process. Susan Hall (2009a) suggests that for a school district of 19 schools in which 13 of the schools are elementary schools, a typical initial exploration team for research and review might include:

- Two elementary principals
- One middle school principal
- The curriculum director at the district office
- The special education district coordinator

The implementation team should also include instructional leaders from special education, general education, and Title I during planning of the actual system of interventions. This broader team will determine the types of programs that are needed, how they will be implemented, who will be involved, and required resources (including people and time as well as material resources). This team also will conduct needs assessments of current programs and select a decision-making method for transferring students to different tiers.

Once the implementation team decides that the staff is ready for building an RTI plan, other teams may be formed with specific duties toward the plan, or the original committee may add members as needed to hone the implementation plan.

Phase One: Research and Review

In this phase, team members should gather articles and books on response to intervention and attend workshops and conventions on the topic. To the extent possible, team members should visit sites where RTI has been successfully implemented. They will also take the following steps.

Raise Awareness

RTI is not the responsibility of the special education department; *all* teachers and other school staff have a stake in getting the planning phase right, and parents will also want to understand the new program. Therefore, prior to implementing RTI, it is important for the school or district to conduct awareness meetings for staff and parents to examine the purpose and principles of an RTI program, to compare those to the intervention programs already in place, and to discuss the issues involved in planning and implementing RTI. The team should prepare brochures, PowerPoint presentations, and other materials to help all stakeholders make informed decisions about the type of RTI program that best fits the school. Presentations should be tailored for parents, staff, board members, and administration. For example, for parents, the presentation should include the legal basis and why RTI is better for kids. The presentation for teachers should be more in depth, with a discussion on how RTI programs are implemented, including a sample implementation schedule. Following are some key issues that stakeholder meetings should cover.

- **Definition of RTI and its essential components—** Chapter 1 discussed the components that, at minimum, must be a part of any RTI plan. Emphasis must be on prevention of academic failure through a tiered process of increasingly intensive interventions that are monitored and adjusted frequently to determine and resolve the true source of a child's learning difficulty.

- **How RTI ties to special education eligibility—**An effective RTI plan should be about special education eligibility *and* about closing gaps in learning for all students. As we have seen, in the past, despite good efforts, schools and individual educators made mistakes, such as identifying students as having learning problems when the real problem was an education system that operated as if sociocultural differences did not exist. At the same time, schools have missed students who should have had early interventions, because officials waited for students to fail before offering them help. RTI demands that special education and general education work together to see that no child who needs intervention is missed and that no child is incorrectly placed in a program.

- **Basis of RTI in federal laws, especially IDEA and NCLB legislation**—Several laws have made promises that must be fulfilled. Before educators can accurately assess learning difficulties, schools must take a critical look at curricula and instructional practices. Are students being taught by highly qualified teachers who have been empowered with professional development on best instructional practices and how to execute them correctly to meet the needs of each student?

- **The need to close RTI gaps from the beginning**—Further, because previous intervention programs have not served all students equitably, as chapter 2 showed, schools need to examine whether they have closed RTI gaps by understanding the cultures of the students and by modifying practices accordingly.

- **The significance of schoolwide implementation**—A comprehensive RTI model includes all stakeholders, not only special education staff. Furthermore, a schoolwide plan should not leave to chance who will be responsible at each stage of implementation.

- **A common language**—Fidelity in the planning process requires that everyone understand and use common terminology. Some important terms are listed in the glossary on pages 135–138.

Because RTI requires a systemwide commitment from all educators, it is critical that all staff understand the program and their roles at each tier. Be sure that your planning process results in shared knowledge throughout the school.

Assess the Current Instructional Program

This step should examine important data on student success rates under the instructional program in place. The data should be broken down by ethnicity, gender, special programs, and socioeconomic status as well as by subject area. If behavior is to be included in the first phase of implementation, disaggregated data on numbers of referrals for discipline should also be analyzed. Examine these data to determine if failures occur more often with poor children, with males, or with certain racial groups. If so, ask why.

Analyze Referrals to Special Education

Analyze current referrals to existing programs, again disaggregating data by ethnicity, gender, and socioeconomic status to see if the numbers are in sync with the percentages of students from each of these groups in the school and district population. Look especially at referrals for specific learning disabilities or for behavior issues such as ADD or ADHD. If 30 percent of the school population is African American, and 50 percent of the referrals for SLD are for African American students, then there probably is a problem within the general education program; instructional practices might not be modified for culture. If 50 percent of the student population is male, yet 75 percent of the students referred for behavioral issues are male, then that should send a red flag to the team that teachers may not have been trained effectively on how to work with male students.

Examine the Needs and Priorities of the School or District

To determine how RTI would improve student success, the team must examine whether the current method of referring students for special education services is working, and whether the numbers realistically reflect the student population. Examine your school improvement plan, and determine if going to RTI will help you to meet the goals of your school and district. Going to RTI is a complex process that takes work and time, but if it is better for kids, then it is worth it.

Evaluate the Readiness Level of Staff

Some of the issues that must be addressed at this level include:

- Does the staff currently use research-based methods of instruction that are proven to have high effect sizes on student learning?

- Is the curriculum aligned with state and national standards?

- Are the formative and summative assessments used in the classroom in line with the local, state, and national goals for instruction?

- What is the background knowledge of the staff in terms of RTI?

- What is the attitude of the staff regarding an implementation plan?

Identify Screening Instruments and Processes

The next step is to identify what kinds of instruments will be used to screen all students at the beginning of the implementation, who will be responsible for the universal screening, and what kinds of data are needed to determine the learning level of students. Universal screening will provide critical baseline data so that data-based decisions can be made in regard to what constitutes a gap in learning. Schools that do not currently have a screening instrument in place will need to select one at this time. According to Hall (2009a), "Most districts start RTI with reading, or reading combined with behavior. One of the reasons reading is selected over math is that curriculum-based measurements (CBMs) are more readily available. Most likely, the district will select a CBM such as the Dynamic Indicators of Basic Early Literacy Skills (DIBELS) or AimsWeb for universal screening." The tool selected is usually given three times yearly to determine which students are not reaching the benchmarks for their grade level.

Phase Two: Creating an RTI System

Once the team has thoroughly researched and reviewed the elements of RTI, the team will ensure that a written plan is in place before implementation. By this time, staff should believe that RTI is important to students and that it will lead to greater student success. The team should also expand to include staff members important to the implementation of RTI: special education teachers, general education teachers, Title I teachers, speech-language pathologists, English as a second language teachers, literacy specialists, and curriculum specialists, and others as needed. This expanded team is critical to the success and seamless integration of the RTI program within the general education program. Some of the decisions that a team must make at this level of the planning, according to Hall (2009b), include:

- **Staffing**—Who will provide the intervention instruction?

- **Assessment tools**—Do we need to purchase or license any?

- **Curriculum inventory**—What do we have, and what will we need?

- **Administrative leadership**—What steps do the leaders need to take to support this initiative?

- **Teacher training**—What kind of support, coaching, or professional development will be needed?

- **Teacher background knowledge**—What exists and what will we need to provide?

- **Budget/funding**—How much may be needed, and what are the potential funding sources?

Additional decisions that must be made at this point in the planning (Hall, 2009b) include the following.

Select a Service Delivery Method

The most important decisions in RTI implementation will be when to start an intervention, when to continue it for a longer time, when to increase its intensity to the next tier, when to discontinue it, and when to evaluate a student for special education eligibility. Schools use either a *standard protocol* or *problem-solving model* for making these decisions (Fuchs, Mock, Morgan, & Young, 2003). Both structures have as their goal to provide additional help to students who are struggling, and in both methods, the effectiveness of the current intervention is evaluated based on progress-monitoring data to determine how and when to continue, drop, or modify them. How the two methods approach selecting an intervention differs, however. The standard protocol method relies on one consistent intervention, selected by the school, to address a need shared by multiple students. The problem-solving model relies heavily on a problem-solving team of educators who are responsible for analyzing the data on students, authorizing further assessments if needed, and then brainstorming possible strategies for intervention based on individual needs. This team is also responsible for seeing that follow-up data are analyzed to determine if students are progressing adequately after the interventions.

 In both the problem-solving model and standard treatment protocol, universal screening takes place at the onset, all students receive high-quality instruction, and progress monitoring is conducted to determine performance levels and rates of improvement for students. Both have been shown to be validated methods of working with students who are struggling in the classroom. The major difference between the two approaches lies in what happens whena student is not making progress at Tier 1 (see table 3.1).

Standard Protocol

The standard protocol model assumes that students with similar academic or behavioral needs will respond to the same empirically validated intervention. It is sometimes referred to as a

Table 3.1: Intervention Methodologies

Problem-Solving Model	Standard Protocol
A team makes the instruction decision by first identifying the problem and its cause and then developing a plan to address the problem.	The person delivering the instruction makes the decisions following a prescribed protocol defined in the planning phase.
A variety of interventions are presented that address the skill gaps identified.	Students with similar skill gaps are presented with the same research-validated intervention.
Interventions are individualized and may change based on the student's response to the intervention.	The intervention (presented to a number of students at the same time) addresses multiple skill sets.

Source: IRIS Center, 2007a.

"quality control" method of intervening. All interventions called standard protocol interventions should have a research base that includes how the protocol was implemented at the experimental stage, for how long, and how many times; this information tells educators how to implement the protocol with fidelity to ensure that they obtain the same results.

For example, all students having difficulty with phoneme blending might be placed in a group together where they receive validated best-practice strategies in phoneme blending. Maanum (2009) suggests this strategy for helping students with phoneme blending:

> Use letter cubes, magnetic letters, letter tiles, or any other type of manipulative to spell a word. . . .
>
> Say the word *cat* and have the child repeat the word back to you. Next, the teacher will model by saying the sounds in cat and while saying the sounds, push the appropriate tile or cube up on the table: /c/ /a/ /t/. Have the child repeat the word after you. (p. 174)

If you are using the standard protocol intervention method, this strategy (or any other strategy designated by your RTI teams in the planning phase) would be *the* strategy applied to all students having difficulty with phoneme blending.

Problem-Solving Model

The problem-solving model assumes that no single strategy will work for all students with the same problem. Under this model, RTI teams use data to identify problems, analyze them, and create a plan for implementation and evaluation. This plan is sensitive to the differences in individual students in terms of background knowledge, access to quality instruction, learning styles, and modalities.

Under this approach, a problem-solving team is established that will assist the classroom teacher and other instructional staff with decisions about students who are not successful in the regular classroom setting. Using data and a scientific approach to problem solving, this team identifies the learning problem, observes and measures the problem in the regular classroom setting, and develops a hypothesis about the cause of the problem. Based on their findings, the team makes recommendations for evidence-based strategies to apply to the learning problems. Once the strategies are in place, the team measures progress at designated intervals of time to determine effectiveness of the strategies. The team makes a determination of whether to continue the intervention, change it, or refer the student for more intense interventions.

According to the National Research Center on Learning Disabilities (2007), the following characteristics are essential when implementing a problem-solving approach:

- A scientific approach to problem solving

- Interventions designed for an individual student

- A system for continual monitoring and evaluation of intervention

- Collaborative relationships with general education and special education to develop, implement, and monitor the intervention

■ Collections of information from a variety of sources including teachers, parents, and others who best know the child

■ Use of curriculum-based measurement (CBM) to assist in problem identification, continuing progress monitoring, and evaluation of the effectiveness of the intervention

■ Interventions embedded in the daily classroom routine so the classroom teacher takes responsibility for implementation

Problem solving often is depicted by a visual diagram such as the one provided in figure 3.1.

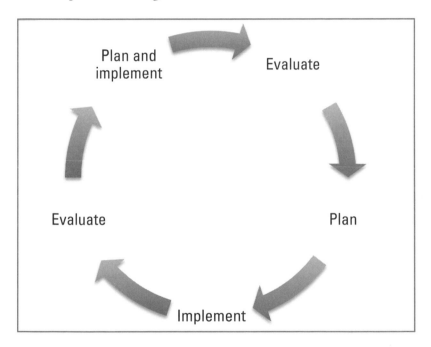

Figure 3.1: The problem-solving approach.

In defining the problem, an intervention team will examine gaps between actual and expected performance of individual students and groups based on universal screening. At this point, this is a precaution that says to the educator that there may be a problem and further assessment and review should be taken. The team will look at research-based instructional practices to help determine whether the universal screening results are the result of inappropriate instruction or arise from other causes.

If a skill gap does exist, the team will select research-based strategies for intervention and methods for tracking learners' progress. All of this information needs to be specific and written so that all educators are aware of the interventions that are part of the schoolwide plan.

The intervention team will be responsible for ensuring that interventions are carried out with fidelity. This team also will be responsible for ongoing monitoring of both the processes and students' progress. Guidelines should be in place to help educators make sound decisions about when to fade, continue, or change an intervention. This is true for both academic and behavioral interventions. The intervention team will conduct ongoing evaluation by gathering data to determine whether an intervention has been successful and, if not, why not. The team will make changes according to their evaluation of these data, and the cycle will repeat.

Decide Who Will Teach the Interventions at Each Tier

During the planning phase, the implementation team will also need to decide who will be responsible for delivering interventions. The selection of those teachers (and their advisors) responsible for the interventions at each tier is critical. If the general education teacher will be responsible for the interventions and their documentation, will that teacher have support staff to help? Who will evaluate the program and ensure that it is carried out with fidelity?

Decide Where Students Will Be Served

By Tier 2, the classroom teacher, specialists, or aides may decide to take small groups to a quieter area of the classroom for supplemental instruction. Tier 3 usually occurs outside of the general education classroom. The decision is completely the decision of the schools and is based on staff and availability of space, but should be made during planning so that all know what to expect.

Decide When Students Will Be Served

When students are served is a critical question. Based on the studies of hundreds of RTI programs, Susan Hall (2009b) says that those schools who specify a block of time for interventions at Tiers 2 and 3 appear to have success earlier than those who do not. The rationale is that students need more time on the subject area, not less—that is, they need to participate in their regular classroom instruction and then receive interventions on targeted skills separately.

Decide How Students Will Be Assessed at Tiers 2 and 3

Once the screening instrument has been chosen for the general population, the next step is to determine how student progress after interventions will be tracked and how often. There are several assessments that schools can purchase. Many schools are moving toward creating their own assessments since doing so ensures that students are being assessed on what they have actually been taught rather than relying on assessments that may or may not be mapped to the instructional program. However a school chooses to assess, assessments should be completed often enough to determine if students are making adequate progress and if they are making progress at a rate that will ensure that they will meet their learning goals. For example, a student who shows gaps in understanding text will need to be assessed on that process skill at regular intervals and for a long enough period of time to determine if he or she is on track to close the achievement gap. If the student is making slow progress, no progress, or negative progress, then changes will need to be made, either by trying a new intervention at the current tier or moving the student to the next tier for more intensive intervention. If the student is making progress that is greater than expected or has already met the goal, then a determination will need to be made as to whether the student can successfully return to a lower tier or whether the student needs more time at the present tier with a more aggressive goal.

Avoiding Common Pitfalls

In her article on getting started in RTI, Susan Hall (2009c) lists eleven pitfalls that schools often encounter in preparing to implement response to intervention. Following are suggestions to help guide decisions during planning and thus avoid the pitfalls Hall identifies.

Pitfall 1: Underestimating the Magnitude of Change

Response to intervention involves a change in the way teachers view students, effective teaching, and assessment. This type of change requires studying research and talking to others who are implementing RTI within the school or district. It involves taking a hard look at curriculum, including how and when various topics are taught, and correctly monitoring instructional failures. Planning incorporates effective, ongoing staff development. It means truly examining every child for strengths and weaknesses, and then using proven instructional practices that take into account the culture of the students: how they learn and whether learning problems arise from nonacademic issues, such as a poverty environment or compromised health.

Pitfall 2: Taking on Too Many Grade Levels, Tiers, or Buildings in the First Year

Most types of change require time. Educators should be realistic about the time and personnel RTI will take. Schools that jump in without careful analysis of problems in the current program and how to make changes may simply replicate those problems in a new program. Based on her research with schools that have implemented RTI, Susan Hall (2009c) suggests that schools start with only a few grade levels and gradually phase in the others over time. By using a phased-in program, staff will have the time to gain experience and confidence about what works and what does not.

Pitfall 3: Jumping in Without a Comprehensive Implementation Plan

Without a plan, staff changes or discouragement can sabotage the change process. With a comprehensive plan, implementation can be carried out regardless of staff changes, because it is based on a thoughtful process. The first step in that process should be to determine the areas of weakness in the current program by looking at existing data and asking some hard questions, such as:

- Do the achievement data show possible anomalies, such as a high percentage of economically disadvantaged children in special education programs?

- Do the data show a disproportionate number of African American males in special education programs for learning disabled, attention deficit disorder, or attention deficit hyperactive disorder?

- Are the assessments currently used for determining these programs biased in terms of cultural differences in learning?

- What percentage of students placed in programs such as learning disabled are later moved back into the mainstream?

- What percentage of minority students placed in these special education programs graduate from high school?

- Have best practices been modified for culture and poverty?

Determining the answers to these questions will not only show where your RTI program should focus, but also build a sense of urgency among staff to address identified problems.

Pitfall 4: Failing to View the Implementation as a Systemwide Change

RTI is the responsibility of everyone on staff, from the secretary in the school office to the classroom teacher. Schools are about creating a high-quality education for every child, and everyone who is an employee of the school is a part of the process. Including all employees is part of the awareness phase. Parents and school board members also should be invited to participate in awareness meetings. Every community has outspoken parents to whom others listen; these parents can be the best supporters of change if they are invited to be part of the process.

Pitfall 5: Failing to Designate an Intervention Block Time in the Master Schedule

Teachers are short on time, and so the implementation plan must ensure that adequate time is provided for teachers to understand the process, to study and discuss new ideas, and to review assessments on an ongoing basis. By designating an intervention block separate from the regular classroom time spent on reading and math, students do not lose direct instruction in the basic skills that they need to be successful. Some schools have a separate time in the daily schedule for interventions that take place at a time when basic skills are not being taught. Other schools have carved out time for interventions during that time in the classroom when other students are working on assignments, other skills, or homework.

Pitfall 6: Focusing on Collecting Assessment Data Rather Than on Learning to Use the Data

Educators often talk about students' self-efficacy—students' belief that they can successfully do a given task based on past positive and successful experiences. The same is true for teachers. They need motivation to spend the time and energy necessary to make RTI work. Teachers need to understand why RTI is better for kids and how it will lead to greater success in the classroom.

Pitfall 7: Viewing Purchased Instructional Programs as Silver Bullets

Students and cultures come in many variations. Educators need to ensure that interventions are relevant to their own students. What works for a school that is predominately white and middle class may not work in a school with a different cultural or socio-economic situation. There are cultural differences in the ways that students—and teachers—learn. Purchased interventions are tools to help well-trained teachers make informed instructional decisions, not panaceas.

Many sources now provide research-based packages to help teachers intervene and track RTI programs. The National Center on Response to Intervention (www.rti4success.org) is a good source of information on available programs.

Pitfall 8: Forming Groups Based on a Surface View of the Data

Achievement data alone are not sufficient for some decisions about implementation. What else do teachers know about their students? For example, has the school or have individual teachers done climate surveys to determine what individual students like to do, what they think of school, and so on? By learning about students and their background knowledge, we can first be sure that the learning is personally relevant and second lead students to projects that have meaning and interest to them.

Pitfall 9: Over-Relying on CBM Data Instead of Organizing an Assessment System

Curriculum-based measurements use cut-off points to assist teachers and other educators to determine if a student is potentially at risk. After interventions have been employed, graphs of results help to determine if students are responding to the interventions appropriately. CBMs have been used for two decades to track student progress through multiple tests. But CBMs need to be analyzed in terms of the student population to ensure that they take students' background knowledge into consideration; they should not be used alone when poverty may be an issue. For example, a cut-off score of fifty words read correctly within a given point of time is a good measure—as long as you know that the vocabulary does not contain bias by geographic area or ethnicity. A picture of a sled with the word *toboggan* is all right in New England, but in Texas, where I live, a toboggan is a hat.

Pitfall 10: Confusing Awareness Training With Implementation Training

Awareness training is general and informs the staff and others about RTI and the implementation steps. It also should emphasize benefits and pitfalls so that staff can make informed decisions from the beginning. *Implementation* training is specific and acts as both a heuristic and an algorithm to ensure success of the program; it should be a systemic, in-depth process that explains how response to intervention will be carried out at each tier.

Pitfall 11: Training Teachers on the Wrong Things

Training should be carefully selected, based on identified needs and learning gaps that were determined during the planning phase. Can teachers implement the objectives in the comprehensive plan? For example, if the planning phase found that a disproportionate number of African American males had been identified as learning disabled, then what training would enable teachers to analyze whether such placements are correct? Training should always be matched to the practices that have to be changed. Simply providing more training on a random topic, however good the training is, will not affect the outcomes that matter.

Table 3.2 is an example of how an RTI committee might document how it will handle the problem described earlier: a disproportionate number of African American males identified as at risk. Under "Objective Defined in Comprehensive Plan," the committee re-evaluates the issue of possible bias in the testing process and/or the instructional program. Step One is examining the data for trends that might indicate possible issues with test or curriculum bias. In Step Two, the committee recommends that the staff receive training in identifying areas of test bias and areas of the curriculum and instructional program that may not be culturally competent. In Step Three, teachers will use the tactics learned in the training to provide a culturally relevant instructional program. In Step Four, educators in the building or district responsible for curriculum and instruction will ensure that curriculum, instruction, and assessments are modified for culture and for poverty as appropriate.

Table 3.2: A Plan for Closing RTI Gaps

Objective Defined in Comprehensive Plan	Eliminate bias in selection process.
Step One	Understand the existing data, and be able to identify areas of possible weakness in the process.
Step Two	Receive training on diversity.
Step Three	Employ tactics in the classroom that teach to the culture of the students.
Step Four	Use research based instructional practices that have been modified for culture and poverty.

Pitfall 12: Not Taking Into Account the Culture of the Students

To Hall's original list of eleven pitfalls, I would add this twelfth pitfall. We have learned that culture affects both teaching and learning. Ignoring that issue is the problem at the very heart of why we are placing minorities and children from poverty into special education in disproportionate numbers. Table 2.1 (page 48) is a starting point for understanding some differences in how various cultures may view the world and education. The RTI plan must address how the instructional program will be modified to address these differences.

In Conclusion

Teachers and administrators face a number of important issues as they make decisions about how to create an RTI model that achieves its goals. This chapter has examined some of these key issues, along with some common pitfalls reported by schools that already have implemented RTI programs.

Learning Log

In this chapter	Your thoughts
In this chapter, we looked at some of the responsibilities of the team that will be planning and later implementing the RTI program. What is a key issue with your current intervention program that you hope to avoid in a new RTI program?	
In the next chapter	
In the next chapter, we will discuss Tier 1 of the RTI model. What kinds of preassessment data do you currently collect on your students? Can you point to scientifically based instructional practices that you use regularly in your classroom?	

Chapter four

Closing the Gap at Tier 1

A basic goal of any RTI program is prevention and early support for learning problems revealed in universal screenings. Schools prevent learning problems by making sure that all children are taught by highly qualified teachers who know and use best practices, know how to modify instruction for culture and poverty, and use research-based practices and materials. Teachers provide early supports by gathering and analyzing student screening data and then making changes in instruction at the first sign that current methods are not working. This core preventative curriculum is typically called Tier 1 in the RTI model. It requires regular screening for academic and behavior issues, differentiated instruction that addresses those issues, and regular progress monitoring to ensure that the differentiated instruction is meeting all needs.

Tier 1 is sometimes referred to as the universal level. Tier 1 screening combines resources from the staffs of general education, special education, and Title I to gather data (through testing and observations) about the achievement of every student, based on identified benchmarks for subjects and grade levels. Included are state and local benchmarks for both academics and behaviors. Key questions include: Are students making the academic and behavioral progress expected for this grade or subject? Are students making adequate yearly progress? If not, what skills do students need, and how can teachers modify instruction so that students can succeed? Differentiated instruction should be part of the daily teaching and learning process in whole-class and small-group instruction. If educators spend adequate time and attention on solving problems at the planning stage, then they will have identified best practices that will be needed to ensure students' success and embedded those into the teaching process. This chapter will explore how educators can ensure their Tier 1 RTI program is implemented to ensure the success of all students—to close the gap from the outset.

Monitoring the Strength of the Core Curriculum

As stated earlier, the research on Tier 1 suggests the guidelines of 80–15–5 often used in medical or public health models; educators can expect that 80 percent of the students in the general education classroom will be successful. According to the IDEA Partnership (2007a):

> Where the general education instruction is successful, it is widely accepted that 15 percent of students struggle with isolated skills and/or concepts at points throughout the year. And approximately 5 percent of the student population will be in need of the most intensive interventions to access and progress in the curriculum. (p. 15)

If fewer than 80 percent of students are successful in the general education classroom, then a school may need to consider more systemic changes in teaching practices before initiating RTI interventions at Tiers 2 and 3. In other words, educators should go back to the planning table to ensure that basic content and pedagogy are sound and research based before creating interventions. The tenets of Tier 1 should be addressed and analyzed often. Following are useful questions to guide this analysis:

1. Have teachers been trained to recognize and implement best practices? Best practices are instructional methods that are proven to be effective on student learning. Efficacy of such methods often is stated in terms of effect sizes, which can be converted to percentiles.

2. Do teachers know how to modify instruction for culture and poverty?

3. Do teachers have adequate reports from state tests so that they can identify specific areas of weaknesses exhibited by individual students or groups of students?

4. Do teachers know how to interpret the standards for their state and local schools to determine what students need to know and be able to do and at what level?

5. Do teachers know the importance of vocabulary to high-stakes testing and instructional differentiation?

6. Do assessments really test what is important?

7. Do assessments contain biases that may skew test scores?

8. Does the school have a high-quality curriculum, and do teachers know how to implement it?

9. Is fidelity an important part of the program?

10. Do schools and teachers have the resources they need?

In a classroom of 22 students, for example, we would expect that at some point many of the students will periodically need reteaching or clarification without further problems. Some will have learning gaps that will be filled in a short period of time by the regular classroom teacher using classroom resources. Figure 4.1 (page 76) breaks down the learning results for a typical classroom of 22 first-grade students. Of the 22 students, we would anticipate that the learning needs of 15 percent of the class or 3 students will not be satisfied at Tier 1 and that those students will need more specific interventions at Tier 2. Out of those 3 students, we would anticipate that 5 percent of the original class or 1 student might need the more intense interventions at Tier 3. In a typical three-tier RTI model, students who do not make progress at Tier 3 are evaluated for special education services.

At each level where interventions are employed, methods are in place to track the progress of the student and to make decisions to change, cease, or redirect the modifications, based on the progress of the student.

Tier 1: 22 Students (100 percent are screened and given high-quality instruction)

Tier 2: 3 Students (15 percent are assisted in small groups with specific interventions that are monitored for effectiveness)

Tier 3: 1 Student (5 percent are provided individual and more intense interventions that are monitored for effectiveness)

Figure 4.1: Typical classroom breakdown of students served by RTI tiers.

Tier 1 of a multitier model is crucial to the success of the entire program because it is in this tier that all students should be provided scientific, research-based instruction by a highly qualified teacher who uses universal screening and progress monitoring to determine student needs and progress. However, as we learned in chapter 2, culture plays an enormous role in student success. For that reason, it is essential that teachers differentiate their core instruction in general education classrooms in light of what we know about learning preferences and cultural biases. The best instructional strategy in the world is only as good as those who implement it.

Suppose your school has decided to create an intervention model based on the principles of response to intervention and has created teams among faculty and staff to plan for implementation. How can you modify best practices for the cultures within your classrooms? Effective teachers do not use different instructional strategies for different cultures. Rather, they use identified best practices that are modified for cultural differences.

Appropriate responses to the needs of students in poverty must be based on knowledge of the students. Teachers need to understand the culture of their students, including how students view education and prefer to learn, the importance of collaboration, the kinds of experiences students bring to school, and students' vocabulary knowledge. Teachers of English learners must assess and take into account their students' English proficiency. Teachers must move away from a model that looks at students in poverty as individuals who need to be "fixed." Instead, teachers must adopt a model that looks first at students' strengths and then fills knowledge and experience gaps through appropriate scaffolding of instruction. Teachers can close the RTI gap from the outset by building relationships first, focusing on vocabulary, differentiating instruction, and teaching to reach all systems of thinking.

Building Relationships First

Remember that for most cultures of the world, including cultures within the African American and Mexican American communities, positive teacher-student relationships must be established before the substance of the curriculum is taught. Until a good teacher-student relationship is established, high-quality teaching and learning may not take place. This tends to be the opposite of the traditional North American classroom model, in which teaching comes first and teachers create relationships along the way.

Most North American teachers today are white females. What difference does that make? Early indicators are that many white female teachers have not been trained to recognize and accommodate factors that affect learning by students in nondominant cultures. Furthermore, these teachers often are distressed when students from other cultures do not pay attention or show hostility toward the teacher.

Effective teachers ensure that students know they all compose a community of learners, and teachers learn along with their students. The goal is not "teacher and curriculum versus students" but students and teachers tackling the curriculum together. For example, I knew a first-grade student who struggled throughout the year and was unhappy about going to school. However, his wise second-grade teacher knew about creating relationships and told her students, "I want you to do your very best work, but if you just can't figure out the work, let me know, and I will sit by you so we can figure it out together." The little boy who had been so unhappy in first grade smiled when he told me, "She does what she said. She sits by me and helps me figure it out." He started thriving in school, and there were no more tears before class. Teachers who are good at creating this type of inviting learning environment regard children from poverty or other cultures as bringing individual gifts to the learning situation. An inviting learning community communicates that students can accomplish the tasks set before them. Too often students in poverty believe that they have no locus of control; bad things just happen to poor people, they may think. Schools and teachers can help build students' sense of self-efficacy (that they can be successful because they have had success in the past) by using best practices modified for these students' learning needs.

Focusing on Vocabulary

Students from impoverished backgrounds often come to school with half the vocabulary of their white middle-class peers, as we learned earlier (Marzano & Kendall, 1996). In Tier 1, a student may be incorrectly diagnosed with a learning problem when, in fact, the problem actually is lack of opportunity to learn vocabulary. Thus the first strategy should be to expose these students to the vocabulary essential for success at grade level and in given subjects, regardless of whether the students are first-graders or eighth-graders.

Marzano and Kendall (1996) also say that 85 percent of the success on state tests is based on students' knowledge of the vocabulary of the standards. It should be no surprise that students in poverty and English learners tend to score lower on state tests. If a primary measure for determining whether students need interventions is the state test, then schools need to teach the vocabulary of the standards as a first step.

Steps to Teach Vocabulary

How can teachers effectively teach vocabulary? Marzano and Pickering (2005) recommend the following steps.

Step 1: Build background knowledge

Find out what words students already know, and teach the words they do not know or about which they have misconceptions. Several types of visual organizers can help teachers find out what students already know in order to fill any gaps in prior knowledge. Figure 4.2 provides one example.

Word	What I Know	Teacher Definition (working definition)	My Definition (after the learning)	My Graphic
Tall tale	Main character is sometimes big.	A tall tale is a fictional story that began as a true story about a person or object and then was exaggerated over time so that the characters or object took on "larger than life" characteristics.	A fictional story that uses humor and exaggeration; began as a true story that was added to as people passed the story along.	T
Fantasy	Not true			
Myth	A moral			

Figure 4.2: Vocabulary organizer to assess and build background knowledge.

In the first column, students are given the word or words that they will need to know. In the second column, students provide the teacher with their background knowledge on the word or word.

It's important to remember that Marzano and Kendall's research centers on the importance of the vocabulary in the standard, in particular. Figure 4.3 (page 80) shows a typical fifth-grade standard and benchmark for reading.

Identifies the forms of fiction and describes the major characteristics of each form.

Knows the defining characteristics of various genres (i.e., fiction, nonfiction, myths, poems, fantasies, biographies, science fiction, autobiographies, tall tales, supernatural tales).

Figure 4.3: Standard for reading.

As a teacher, I would not assume that any of my students already know any of these words. Instead, I would use a graphic organizer such as that in figure 4.4 to determine which words my students already know.

Word	I have never seen this word before.	I have seen this word, but I don't know its meaning.	I am familiar with the word and know its meaning.
Defining characteristic			
Genre			
Fiction			
Nonfiction			
Myth			
Poem			
Fantasy			
Biography			
Science fiction			
Tall tale			

Autobiography			
Supernatural tale			

Figure 4.4: Graphic organizer for assessing background knowledge of vocabulary.

By using a graphic organizer and asking students to check the box that most closely explains their level of background knowledge for each word, the teacher can make informed decisions about the amount of time and the level of vocabulary instruction that the class will need. This is also a way to determine if an individual student or a group of students need additional support on learning vocabulary in Tier 2.

Step 2: Provide a working definition

Providing a working definition of the word or words is another way to give students the background knowledge to understand the lessons. This is not the formal definition that students will eventually learn but rather a preliminary definition to use while the lesson is being taught.

Give students examples of correct and incorrect meanings of target words. English learners will benefit from the use of pictures, graphs, and models. Tileston and Darling (2008) suggest the following as ways to provide a brief explanation and a visual of new words:

- Use direct experiences that provide examples.

- Use a story format.

- Use images.

- Let students teach the term.

- Use current events.

- Ask students to describe their mental pictures of the term.

- Find or create pictures of the term.

- Use something about which students already have some knowledge. For example, the teacher might say, "Look at your milk container, and you will see the word *pasteurized*. That word means that the milk was heated to kill the bacteria that could make you sick. Louis Pasteur, a man from France, invented the process in the 1800s to make milk safe to drink. That process was then named after him."

Step 3: Teach words in context

Words are more meaningful if students know why they are learning them and how the words are used in the real world. Having students look up words in a dictionary and memorize them for a test is an ineffective way to teach vocabulary. During this part of the lesson, students learn about the words in the context of the lesson. Students might read a story about Paul Bunyan and determine why it is considered to be a tall tale rather than a fantasy.

Step 4: Ask students to write definitions in their own words

Information that is personally relevant is easier to recall. Motivation to learn also is partially dependent on the personal meaning of the learning. Have students write a definition in their own words based on what they have learned in the lesson. It is important to put the definition in their own words because we tend to remember best things that are personally relevant to us.

Step 5: Use graphic representations of words

Vocabulary is stored in the semantic memory system, which is the least reliable of human memory systems. To retrieve words from this system, individuals need a hook, or a context, and must have appropriate language skills. English learners in the early stages of proficiency probably will not yet have these skills.

Younger students may benefit from a graphic organizer more like the one shown in figure 4.5.

Teacher Definition	Teacher Drawing
A four-sided figure with all sides equal	
My Definition	My Drawing
Something with four sides that are all the same size	

Figure 4.5: Elementary word organizer for *square*.

Teach Math Vocabulary

Vocabulary is also critical to learning math. Figure 4.6 provides a math example of how a standard might be written. In this example, students at grade 1 are given a list of shapes that they will be expected to recognize.

> Geometric Shapes: Students will recognize and use geometric shapes.
>
> Grade 1: Students will recognize a circle, square, triangle, cube, sphere, and rectangle in real world situations.

Figure 4.6: Grade 1 math standard.

What vocabulary words must students know in order to demonstrate understanding of this standard? They would need to know *circle, square, triangle, cube, sphere,* and *rectangle* so that they could recognize these shapes when they see them. They would therefore need to know the attributes of a circle that make it a circle instead of a sphere or a rectangle. One would assume that students will be given pictures of shapes which they must identify by their correct name.

Vocabulary is also critical at the secondary level; math scores there can also be increased by first teaching the vocabulary of math. For example, a teacher gives the following problem:

In the expression 7*a*:

1. What is the coefficient?

2. What is the variable?

If students do not know the definitions of *coefficient* and *variable*, then they will not know the answers. On the other hand, a teacher might translate math talk into English, especially for new concepts. The teacher might provide information along the lines of figure 4.7.

Word	Definition	Discussion
Variable	In algebra, a letter is often used to stand for a number. The letter used to stand for a number is called a variable. You can use any letter, but *a*, *b*, *c*, *n*, *x*, *y*, and *z* are the most commonly used letters.	$x + 3 = 5$ x is the variable. $a - 2 = 6$ a is the variable. $5z = 10$ z is the variable. $x + y = 7$ Both x and y are variables.
Coefficients	The coefficient is the number in front of the variable.	$x + 3 = 5$ 1 is the coefficient. $5z = 10$ 5 is the coefficient.

Figure 4.7: Organizer for math vocabulary.

With this information at the outset, answering the questions becomes much easier because students know what the terms mean. Notice that I have not watered down the learning but have simply provided students with scaffolding (the structure of a matrix) to help them understand. By teaching with scaffolding, we can teach at high levels and close gaps at the same time.

We have discussed two of the most critical and often overlooked areas of modification for culture and poverty; namely, creating relationships and teaching vocabulary first. Table 2.1 (page 48) shows that outside of the students from a Northern European background, all other cultures of the world need the teacher to create a relationship first and then provide the substance of the learning. By doing this up front, teachers are more likely to have students on board from the beginning. By teaching vocabulary first, we are assured that students who may not have the background knowledge expected for their age and grade level will more likely be successful in the classroom. Never assume that your students know the vocabulary of the subject area; find out and directly teach the vocabulary needed to participate in the learning at a high level. In the sections that follow, we will examine some other important ways to differentiate the learning.

Differentiating Instruction

When teaching children from poverty and diverse cultures, the goal is not to use different instructional strategies, but to modify best practices. Modifications are created in three ways: (1) differentiating for context, (2) differentiating for content and product, and (3) differentiating for process.

Differentiate for Context

When teachers differentiate for context, they create culturally responsive classrooms for students of color and students from poverty. They respond to the atmosphere of a classroom—not just socially, but also through instructional presentation. Creating a culturally responsive classroom incorporates three major strategies (Shade, Kelly, & Oberg, 1997). These strategies—explicit feedback, cooperative learning, and wait time—can be described within the broad context of an inviting learning environment. Table 4.1 (page 86) describes these methods and their impact on learning.

Table 4.1: Differentiation for Context

Instructional Method	Description	Effect Size	Percentile Point Gain
Giving explicit feedback	Tell individual students specifically what they are doing well, and make specific recommendations for improvement.	1.13	37
Using cooperative learning	Use the principles of cooperative learning to provide practice time for the new learning.	0.77	28
Extending wait time	Provide adequate and consistent amounts of time for students to answer questions.	1.28	40

Effect sizes from Tileston & Darling, 2009.

Explicit feedback

Researchers have found that providing explicit feedback, the first strategy in differentiating for context, raises average student scores by 37 percentile points (Tileston & Darling, 2009). Many teachers say that they practice explicit feedback, but a close examination reveals a variety of interpretations of explicit feedback. We will only get the gains cited in the research if we use the instructional practice as it was used in the research study. For example, simply saying "good job" or "way to go" is not what the researchers meant when they cited positive feedback as having a high effect size on student learning. Giving explicit feedback tells students exactly what they are doing correctly and provides ideas for improvement. In the studies recording a 37 percentile point difference, the feedback was more like this: "I like your opening sentence; it grabs me and makes me want to read more. Your next paragraph, however, is better suited for later in your essay, after you have explained to your audience why they should care about the topic." In this example, the teacher praised the specific piece that was good and provided feedback on how to make it better. This is very different than a blanket statement such as "good job."

Cooperative learning

The second strategy that is highly effective is cooperative learning. In the chart provided in chapter 2 (table 2.1, page 48) on the differences between cultures, we saw that many cultures throughout the world learn collaboratively. This makes cooperative learning important as educators work with various cultures in the classroom. According to Tileston and Darling (2009), cooperative learning can give us an effect size of 28 percentile points. Cooperative learning will not produce this effect size, however, unless it is carried out with all of the elements in place. Johnson and Johnson (2008) designed cooperative learning to contain the following elements:

1. **Positive interdependence**—When this element is in place, students work together toward common goals, and they do that through everyone participating at a high level.

2. **Individual and group accountability**—Every student is individually accountable for the learning and is assessed individually. The group is accountable for participating at a high level and for seeing that all of the elements of the process are in place in their groups.

3. **Face-to-face interaction**—Participants look each other in the eye, lean forward to talk, and are accountable to participate actively in their groups.

4. **Interpersonal and small-group skills**—The skills necessary to work with other people are directly taught and are emphasized along with the cognitive instruction. Students are held accountable for their skills at working with other people.

5. **Group processing**—Evaluation and reflection of their work as a group are a part of the cooperative learning

process. Group processing may be conducted by the teacher, the group members, or both.

Wait time

The third strategy is using wait time, which can be effective if employed consistently. If a teacher allows longer wait time for students to respond during class discussions, it will not go unnoticed. For English learners, wait time is especially valuable. ELs may understand more English than they speak and may be reluctant to speak in class. Give these students time to think and gain confidence about participating in the discussion.

Differentiate for Content and Product

When teachers differentiate for content and product, they create culturally responsive classrooms for students of color and students from poverty. We often think that we do not have control over content, but we can add information that pertains to the culture of our students. Be aware of the music, holidays, and traditions of the cultures represented by your students so that you can incorporate them into the lessons. Products should often be left up to the students so that student culture and talents may be a part of the products that demonstrate their understanding of the learning.

Content

The more relevant to their lives that content is, the more likely it is that students will truly learn and not just memorize information. Students may ask, "What does this have to do with me? When will I ever use this stuff? Why am I learning this?" For this reason, when teaching students from nondominant cultures, it is important for teachers to remember to reference the students' cultures when choosing books, materials, and other elements of the curriculum. This also helps them connect their prior knowledge.

Table 4.2 provides three examples of instructional strategies that differentiate for content and the effect on students' learning that can be expected.

Table 4.2: Differentiation for Content

Instructional Strategy	Description	Effect Size	Percentile Point Gain
Teaching for relevancy	Show students how the learning is relevant to them personally.	1.23	30
Activating prior knowledge	Tap into the gifts that students bring to the table, and build their knowledge base, starting with what they already know.	1.75	46
Using graphic representations	Use visual patterns to help students understand the learning.	2.33	49

Effect sizes from Tileston & Darling, 2009.

Educators further differentiate for content when they teach to students' preferred learning modalities. In fact, Jensen (2003) says that when students repeatedly do not "get it," they will never get it—until teachers teach in the modality that is most comfortable for *students*. Using graphic representations to show patterns, for example, achieves a 49 percentile point gain (Tileston & Darling, 2009). Why? Because those are the ways they have learned since birth; the brain forms patterns for learning in this way. Can students learn in other ways? Yes, but teachers should neither expect them to sit and listen willingly to lectures nor expect satisfactory learning as a result. For some students, the lecture approach simply is not brain friendly. By adding movement and visuals in the classroom, teachers increase the level of learning and simultaneously reduce the need for disciplinary measures.

Product

The types of products that teachers receive from students can be enhanced for all students, particularly those from minorities. Table 4.3 shows the effects of differentiating for product.

Table 4.3: Differentiation for Product

Instructional Strategy	Description	Effect Size	Percentile Point Gain
Praising effort	Tell students what they did correctly, and praise the amount of effort that went into the product.	.80	29
Setting goals with realistic timelines	Have students set personal goals, and provide adequate time for completion of the work.	1.22	39
Teaching heuristics	Directly teach the steps necessary for correctly using a skill.	1.17	38

Effect sizes from Tileston & Darling, 2009.

Teachers can differentiate for product by doing the following:

- Provide a rubric that specifies expectations for the finished product. Use rubrics for everything that is assessed, including homework.

- Provide good and bad examples of products.

- Provide algorithms and heuristics in writing. *Algorithms* are specific rules that we follow when we are expected to get the same answer every time, as in mathematics. *Heuristics* are general rules that we follow when we do not expect to get the same answer every time. For example, suppose students working in groups of three are working on real-world problem solving using a housing shortage in their community as their topic. We would not expect every group to get the same answers, so the teacher provides some general guidelines (heuristics) to help students structure their work. For example, suppose a teacher wants students to create a mindmap of their learning. The teacher provides the general steps used in mindmaps such as: (1) draw a circle in the center of the page that identifies the topic; (2) draw spokes from the center circle to outer circles that indicate the component parts or attributes of the topic; (3) use a different color for each spoke; and (4) use pictures as well as words to represent the component parts.

■ Give students choices of products when appropriate.

Differentiate for Process

Process refers to ways that educators modify experiences and opportunities for processing information so that students can make meaning.

Focusing on teaching a general concept by taking apart its elements can help students process information differently and arrive at a full sense of meaning. For example, a class can identify and discuss the particular attributes of a tall tale to better understand that genre (attributes such as being fictional, outlandish, and funny; having exaggerated characters or place; and being based on a real person or story that has changed with each retelling).

Teaching to Reach All Systems of Thinking

In addition to differentiating for context, content, product, and process, we also need to ensure that we teach to reach all systems of thinking. Robert Marzano (1998) identified the following systems of thinking: the self-system, the metacognitive system, and the cognitive system.

Table 4.4 illustrates three instructional strategies for differentiating for process.

Table 4.4: Differentiation for Process

Instructional Strategy	Description	Effect Size	Percentile Point Gain
Teaching goal setting	Directly teach students how to set personal goals for the learning.	2.33	49
Providing heuristics	Provide students with the general steps to the process—in writing.	1.18	38
Focusing on concept attainment	Use attributes to help students to understand the general concept.	1.34	41

Effect sizes from Tileston & Darling, 2009.

Self-System

Regardless of whether teachers are aware of it, students quickly make decisions about whether they will engage in learning. Some researchers say that this type of decision may be made as soon as the first fifteen seconds of the class. Students ask themselves, "Do I want to do this? How important is this to me personally? Will I be successful?" Because mainstream, middle-class instruction often does not relate well to the learning needs of students from nondominant cultures, for many students, such as those living in poverty, the answers to these questions will be a resounding no. Before students become willing to engage in a learning experience, they must believe that the experience and the learning are important and that they can be successful. This idea can be further examined by looking at the subcategories of Marzano's (1998) self-system:

- *Self-attributes* are students' beliefs about themselves with regard to being able to accomplish a task. Teachers reinforce positive self-attributes by providing step-by-step directions in writing or a rubric that defines specific expectations.

- *Self and others* refers to whether students feel comfortable in the classroom. Do they believe that the class is a collaborative community of learners? This belief is important because in most cultures, students learn by sharing information.

- *Worldview* refers to overall beliefs and values of given cultures.

- *Purpose* revolves around how students answer the question, "What do I see as my purpose in the world?" How students answer this question affects how they will learn and the rigor with which they will attack content.

- *Self-efficacy* is the belief, "I can learn even when the material is difficult, because I have been successful in the past." It is important that students experience success, but it also is important that success be genuine, not the result of a watered-down curriculum.

Of these, self-efficacy is particularly important. It also may be linked to reducing attrition among teachers. Student population demographics are changing and with them, the ways that teachers can best teach the growing number of students in poverty and from nondominant cultures. Teachers must examine their own background knowledge of students' cultures and work to learn about modifications that will increase students' success and boost teachers' own self-efficacy.

A revolution in the science of psychology occurred in the 20th century. As a result, most people are now cognizant of the importance of self-esteem. Earlier generations believed that "bragging on" children might make them think they were better than others or cause them to become self-centered. Then, suddenly, teachers were being directed to make students feel good about themselves. Some educators seem to think that if teachers could only make their students feel good about themselves, then all would be well. Students would learn and excel simply by feeling good about what they could do. In an effort to answer this call, many schools began to water down the curriculum so that more students would experience success. Various new classes were introduced that basically provided simpler versions of curriculum content for students who were not successful in the general classroom. "Math Basics," "English for Special Learners," and similarly titled classes popped up everywhere, with textbooks to support them. Colleges and universities were among the first critics of this new ethos, however, as students entered higher education without the fundamentals to be successful in college-level studies. Thus many colleges and universities also felt forced to introduce noncredit fundamental courses to fill students' knowledge gaps so that the students could then move on to college-level work.

Self-esteem is based, in part, on "I think and I feel"—that is, "I think I can do this" or "I feel good about myself so I will try to do this math [or English or science and so on]." First of all, simply feeling good about oneself does not provide a person with the knowledge and skills to be successful. Second, providing students with watered-down coursework does not make them feel good about themselves. In fact, it produces the opposite result. Schools and policymakers did a disservice to many students by providing inferior education under the guise of increasing students' self-esteem. How is self-efficacy different from feel-good notions of self-esteem? Self-efficacy is based on *facts*, not *hopes*.

Metacognitive System

Once students decide to engage in learning, the metacognitive system takes over. This system asks questions such as, "What are my goals? What strategies will I use to demonstrate learning? How will I adjust my strategy if it does not go well?" Any time teachers assign a process (that is, ask students to do something), students' brains formulate plans to carry out the process. When students do not have a goal, do not know the strategies needed to reach the goal, or do not know how to monitor their own learning, frustration results. Teachers hear comments such as, "This is too hard!" or "I give up!" Three subcategories further explain this system:

- *Goal specification* refers to planning and setting goals. It is important that educators directly teach children from poverty how to do this. Directly teaching goal setting with realistic timelines has a positive effect size of 39 percentile points.

- *Process specification and monitoring* refers to feedback and strategies used to carry out learning. Feedback that is positive and prescriptive has an effect size of 37 percentile points.

- *Disposition monitoring* is feedback by the teacher, a student's peers, or the individual student about how he or she is doing.

Cognitive System

If students are engaged with the topic, understand the goals and how they're progressing, the next step is to engage the cognitive system so that they can complete the learning. The cognitive system interacts with two knowledge domains: declarative knowledge, which includes content information, and procedural knowledge, which consists of skills and processes. These two domains are stored differently in the brain and should be taught differently. For example, declarative information usually is stored in the semantic system of the brain, which is the least reliable pathway for remembering, especially for students who do not have command of English. In order to store and retrieve vocabulary in the semantic memory system of the brain, students must first know the vocabulary and then be able to connect it to other knowledge. Thus, to engage the cognitive system, teachers must activate students' declarative *and* procedural knowledge. Rote memorization is a poor way to teach vocabulary as a result. Educators who have access to the latest research understand that using visual organizers, such as vocabulary grids or attribute wheels, has a greater effect on student learning. Any time teachers can give learning a context, it is more likely that their students will be able to store and retrieve the information reliably.

Monitoring Student Progress

Most learning issues can be alleviated in Tier 1, for up to 80 percent of students, using the strategies described in this chapter. For example, if a student is struggling to remember multiplication tables taught in a prior grade, then the student may simply need additional time for review and practice. If several students do not understand a new concept, then the teacher may simply need to reteach it using new strategies and modalities, focusing heavily on vocabulary, and monitor to ensure that the reteaching was successful for all students. Such things happen every day in classrooms across North America. Good teachers always address specific learning needs. The difference in an RTI model is that any type of difficulty, however brief, is documented and analyzed. Table 4.5 shows a sample form for monitoring comprehension at this level.

At Tier 1, it is critical to evaluate data in light of students' cultures. For example, if a test primarily covers declarative information and requires students to have a command of English and grade-level vocabulary, then teachers cannot reasonably expect English learners (ELs) or students in certain poverty groups to do well on the assessment. If 85 percent of a state test is based on declarative knowledge, then data showing that ELs and certain poverty groups are not doing well should be no surprise (Marzano & Kendall, 1996).

We started this chapter by saying that teachers can close that RTI gap from the outset by building relationships, focusing on vocabulary, differentiating instruction, and teaching to reach all systems of thinking. Even after doing all these things, however, about 20 percent of students will still have some type of learning or behavioral difficulty (Bender & Shores, 2007).

Table 4.5: Sample Monitoring Instrument

Student	Area of Concern	Possible Causes to Consider	Observations	Anecdotal Notes	Data	Actions Taken
Abrams, M.	Listening Compre-hension	Hearing Vocabulary	9/18/09	Asked me to repeat direc-tions twice Struggled with the assignment	Passed hearing test Weekly test demonstrates understanding	After discussing privately, I real-ized he did not understand the word *symmetry* and did not have that word in his former school. After we discussed what the word means, he was able to complete the assignment.

Let's walk a student, Marcus, through a typical Tier 1 scenario. All students in Mr. Powers's general education class are universally screened for reading using a curriculum-based measurement. The CBM assesses performance on reading words correctly at a single point in time, using two alternate assessment forms in the same sitting to ensure accurate data. Mr. Powers averages Marcus's two preassessment scores (52 and 38 words read correctly) to get an average CBM score of 40. The cut-off score for Marcus's age and grade level is 50 words, thus Marcus may be at risk for reading problems. As Mr. Powers teaches throughout the semester, he uses high-quality instruction strategies that are proven to have a high effect size on learning. He differentiates instruction for small groups at various readiness levels revealed through the prescreening and monitors each student's progress at least weekly, using short alternate forms of the reading CBM. In addition, he pays special attention to building relationships, teaches vocabulary explicitly, and uses teaching strategies that engage students in learning through his self-system, metacognitive system, and cognitive system.

Using graphs such as the one in figure 4.8, Mr. Powers graphs each student's scores weekly to determine if he or she is making progress in Tier 1 toward the goals the district has set for reading.

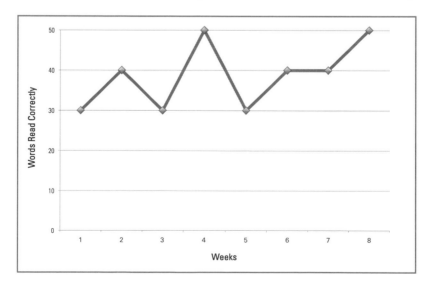

Figure 4.8: Progress monitoring graph in Tier 1 for Marcus.

As time passes, many students respond to the strategies Mr. Powers employs, but Marcus's scores on the CBM still don't consistently pass the cut-off score of 50 words read correctly. After eight weeks, Mr. Powers starts to worry that Marcus will not be able to catch up to his peers by the end of the semester. He decides that Marcus needs supplemental instruction in reading at Tier 2, using a research-based intervention.

In Conclusion

In this chapter, we examined ways to close the RTI gap during Tier 1, through effective core instruction. We examined the importance of building relationships and focusing on vocabulary. We looked at how a teacher might modify context, content, product, and process. We also examined differentiation in terms of systems of thinking, including the self-system, the metacognitive system, and the cognitive system.

In chapter 5, we will examine Tiers 2 and 3 and discuss how the interventions become more intense at these levels.

Learning Log

In this chapter	Your thoughts
In Tier 1, how do you track interventions, and who makes the decisions to move students to Tier 2? What is the basis for moving a student to Tier 2?	
In the next chapter	
In the next chapter, we will discuss how students are moved to Tiers 2 and 3. When might you move a student directly to Tier 3, skipping Tier 2?	

Chapter five

Closing the Gaps at Tiers 2 and 3

As we discussed in chapter 4, when students are found to be at risk for academic or behavioral issues after universal screening, the classroom teacher will typically select and implement research-based instructional strategies to assist those students for those particular issues. When individual students fail to progress successfully within a given timeframe, the teacher (along with other advisors) may determine that the student needs supplemental interventions such as those offered at Tier 2. If the intervention at Tier 2 is successful, it is discontinued or phased out, and the student returns to Tier 1. If it is not successful, the student will progress to Tier 3 to receive more intense and individualized interventions. This chapter will discuss decision making and progress monitoring in Tiers 2 and 3, as well as critical issues in reading and mathematics interventions.

Decision Making

Before moving a student to Tier 2 or Tier 3, the teacher or team should ask the following questions to determine the efficacy of Tier 1 in the particular classroom:

1. Did the student receive research-based instruction that is tied to state and local standards?

2. Did the student receive reading instruction for at least 90 minutes per day? [For elementary teachers]

3. Did the student receive explicit instruction in vocabulary? [For elementary teachers]

4. Were the instructional strategies modified for culture and poverty where appropriate?

5. Have the parents been involved?

The team should also be sure they can answer in the affirmative to the following questions regarding the system as a whole:

1. Did at least 95 percent of the students participate in universal screening?

2. Did the staff receive training on research-based instruction and how to implement it in the classroom?

3. Is there a system in place to measure fidelity of implementation?

4. Is student progress monitored through curriculum-based measurements?

5. Does the team analyze the progress-monitoring results to determine which students are at risk and need more intense interventions?

6. Are data used to inform instructional decision making?

7. Is a clear method in place for collaborating and monitoring students moving from Tier 1 to Tier 2?

Schools should have an established model for (1) determining which students are experiencing difficulties, (2) selecting the appropriate intervention strategies for the individual students, and (3) evaluating the progress of each student. It is expected that as students move along the tiers, the process will become more specific and intense, but it will always follow these three steps.

Document Transitions

Once it has been confirmed that the appropriate measures have been taken in the classroom and in the system to address student learning gaps, then the team must also document transitions between levels. Witt, VanDerHeyden, and Gilbertson

(2004) state that documentation to move students to Tier 2 or Tier 3 should include four components:

1. Student concerns should be clearly and specifically defined.

2. One or more methods of formative assessment should be used to track the effectiveness of the intervention.

3. Baseline student data should be collected prior to the intervention.

4. A goal for student improvement should be calculated before the start of the intervention to judge whether that intervention is ultimately successful.

If a single one of these essential components is missing, the intervention is to be judged as fatally flawed and as not meeting minimum RTI standards. Fuchs, Vaughn, and Fuchs (in press) suggest the following questions be answered at each transition:

- Who is experiencing a problem, and what specifically is the problem?

- What intervention strategies can be used to solve the problem or reduce its severity?

- Did the problem (or problems) go away or decline in severity as a result of the intervention(s)?

Let's examine each of these points in more depth.

Who is experiencing a problem, and what specifically is the problem?

When defining a problem, it is important to clearly describe what the problem "looks like" in objective, observable terms, so that all persons involved know they are talking about the same thing. Measurement of a problem should be direct and occur within the context (classroom setting or situation) in which the problem occurs. To quantify how much of a problem exists, the problem should be described with measurement terms that define frequency, rate, duration, and magnitude. Furthermore, to stay focused on working toward improving problem situations, it is helpful to describe problems as discrepancies between student's actual or current performance (what is) and desired or expected performance (what should be). Thus, in addition to measuring a student's actual performance, criteria regarding expected levels of performance need to be established. By quantifying problems as discrepancies, educators can determine the magnitude or severity of a problem. This information can be useful in formalizing goals (for example, a reduction in the discrepancy) and in prioritizing problems within and across standards.

What intervention strategies can be used to solve the problem or reduce its severity?

When a student has been identified as being in need of intervention, the next step in the self-questioning process is the selection and implementation of appropriate intervention supports, following the school's RTI decision-making method by either choosing the standard protocol for the student's issue or convening a problem-solving team to identify the intervention. There are many intervention strategies from which to choose (visit, for example, www.interventioncentral.com, a website designed to help educators make decisions about research-based interventions).

It is important to identify the factors involved in learning that we can change instructional strategies and curriculum materials as well as pacing. For example, when a child's classroom performance is below grade level, we might ask whether the problem is a skill (*I can't do it*) or a performance (*I won't do it*) problem. Another question to ask is whether the alignment between the student's skill level, the curriculum materials, and instructional strategies is appropriate (Howell & Nolet, 2000). Performance problems can be further narrowed to identify whether the student:

- Does not want to perform the task or activity

- Would rather be doing something else

- Gets something such as attention or access to a preferred activity by not doing the task

- Does not have the prerequisite skills to perform the task

- Is given work that is too difficult or presented in a manner that the student hasn't seen before

- Has been given insufficient time to practice the skill to fluency

For example, if the information we collect suggests that the student has the prerequisite skills needed to decode text but does so slowly, one hypothesis might be that the student has not had sufficient time to practice reading to develop fluency. An appropriate intervention might be to help the student develop fluency by reading practice, such as repeated reading (see Daly & Chrispeels, 2005). If we suspect that the student's problem might be a deficit in pre-reading skills (such as phonemic awareness), our intervention might be to directly teach pre-reading skills with prompting and feedback. In both of these examples, the reading problem was related to a skill issue, and the solutions were related to the type of skill problem (acquisition and fluency). If the information that we gather suggests that the problem is not a skill acquisition but an issue of performance, we may want to first look at why the skill is aversive to the student and then seek ways to make it more interesting or manageable.

Any intervention plan should answer the following questions:

1. What will the intervention look like, including its steps and procedures?

2. What materials or resources are needed, and are they available?

3. What are the roles and responsibilities in regard to running the intervention, such as who is in charge of the intervention, the materials, the assessments, and so on?

4. What is the intervention schedule? Define how often, how long, what time of day, where, and with whom it will be provided.

5. How will the intervention and its outcomes be monitored? What measures, by whom, on what schedule, and analyzed compared to what criteria?

Did the problem (or problems) go away or decline in severity as a result of the intervention(s)?

We will only know a student's response to intervention when a reliable intervention has been implemented and measured repeatedly over time. To determine whether the student's response is appropriate, we must gather information through multiple measures. Progress monitoring is discussed in more depth later in this chapter.

Delivering Interventions

As we have learned, while the purpose of Tier 1 is primarily prevention through the use of differentiation, reteaching, and progress monitoring, Tier 2, or secondary intervention, is for those students who did not respond to the universal core instructional program with its modifications in the regular classroom. To determine which students need Tier 2 intervention, the instructional team will identify a specific cutoff score to indicate content mastery or mastery of specific skills. Students who do not show adequate progress move to Tier 2. These students continue to be a part of the general education classroom but receive supplementary interventions that are specific to the area or areas of need. Usually the instruction is delivered at a specified time in the daily or weekly schedule and is conducted in small groups of two to four students by the general education teacher, a specialist, or trained tutors who may or may not be certified teachers. The number and frequency of the interventions is up to the individual schools or districts and should be specified in their RTI plan.

According to Fuchs, Vaughn, and Fuchs (in press), secondary interventions are usually delivered over a period of 10 to 25 weeks. The interventions at Tier 2 should be research-based and shown to be effective with large numbers of students. As with all interventions, student progress should be carefully monitored and recorded. Through progress monitoring at Tier 2, decisions are made whether the student needs the more intense interventions of Tier 3, whether the interventions need to continue at Tier 2, or whether the student can be placed back in Tier 1.

Bender and Shores (2007) offer some additional guidelines for Tier 2 interventions:

1. When interventions at Tier 1 have not been successful, the general education teacher should confer with other teachers and curriculum specialists to determine the best way to meet the needs of the student.

2. Tier 2 interventions should be offered a minimum of four days a week (this is recommended by Bender and Shores, but the final decision is up to the school or district during RTI planning).

3. Tier 2 interventions should be observed by an administrator or designated specialist to see that the interventions are being conducted with fidelity and in line with the school RTI plan.

4. Parents should be notified when students require Tier 2 interventions.

5. Tier 2 interventions should be assessed using sufficient assessments or data points in order to make an informed decision about whether the intervention is successful.

Again, all decisions should be recorded with appropriate documentation. A classroom teacher who has differentiated instruction in Tier 1 to address needs identified in universal screening scores might send documentation to Tier 2 personnel that looks like figure 5.1 (page 108).

In this case, Marcus was determined to be at risk of reading problems through the *DIBELS* testing that was given to all students in the classroom. His teacher, Mr. Powers, prescribed additional time for Marcus to read aloud and receive tutoring on words that Marcus could not pronounce. Mr. Powers observed that Marcus had difficulty with certain sounds, including some blended sounds. Marcus received six weeks of the appropriate intervention with additional testing each week to determine if the intervention was working and if it was adequate to produce the positive results needed. The second week of testing indicated

	Student: Marcus Walker			Teacher: Tom Powers		
Tier Level	Reason for Intervention	Prescribed Support	Duration	Progress Reviews	Data Results	Recommendation
1	*DIBELS* score for reading was 18.	Additional time for reading aloud with aide and assistance with specific word pronunciation Direct vocabulary instruction	Six weeks with retesting weekly	9/1/10 9/8/10 9/15/10 9/22/10 9/29/10	18 20 18 19 19	Tier 2 interventions for reading in smaller group setting with emphasis on letters /t/ /s/ /r/ and blends Increased reading time

Figure 5.1: Documentation of Tier 1 differentiated instruction based on universal screening.

that Marcus might be making progress, but subsequent testing showed a flat line of improvement.

Decision-Making Tools

Decisions at Tier 2 and Tier 3 are made using data from teacher notes, formative assessments, and progress monitoring of the specific intervention(s) being used. Good progress monitoring can help prevent false positives as well as false negatives. Deciding how to monitor the success of interventions is a critical part of creating a workable model for RTI in any school. Schools use several kinds of online assessments. The *Dynamic Indicators of Basic Early Literacy Skills* (*DIBELS*) has been around for many years and has been used by school personnel to identify possible areas of difficulty and to track progress of students. *Curriculum Management* is another online system that helps schools set cut scores and monitor student progress.

To illustrate this process, consider reading as an example. One measure of "reading health" shown to be predictive of later reading fluency and comprehension is the number of words a student reads correctly per minute, or *oral reading fluency* (Hosp & Fuchs, 2005). *DIBELS* is a research-based, standardized, norm-referenced measure of pre-reading and reading skills that includes a measure of oral reading fluency for grades 1 through 6 (Good, Gruba, & Kaminski, 2002). The *DIBELS* measures were designed for use as screening and evaluation tools, and scores on the *DIBELS* can be used to identify levels of reading risk. Pre-specified, research-based goal rates have been established for *DIBELS* (see http://dibels.uoregon.edu). By comparing actual scores to the suggested cut-off scores, educators can use the data from the universal screening of all students to determine early on who is in need of interventions and at what level.

Let's consider another scenario. Diane Wilson teaches third grade at Montgomery Elementary School, where her students have recently been screened using *DIBELS*. Table 5.1 shows the results for some of her students.

Table 5.1: Student *DIBELS* Results Compared to Cut-Off Score of 77

Student	*DIBELS* Results 9/1/10
Aken, C.	82
Alan, T.	79
Brooks, R.	77
Brunson, Y.	68
Diaz, C.	62
Espinoza, L.	70
Fields, K.	67
Gonzales, P.	30
Graham, J.	38
Jordan, S.	55
Thomas, R.	72
Valez, R.	79
Walker, B.	82
Walker, K.	80
Wilson, T.	35

In this example, the grade 3 *DIBELS* cut-off score for fall testing is 77 words per minute, for the winter term 92 words per minute, and for the spring term 110 or more words per minute. Looking at the table, we see that eight students scored below the cut-off score, and two other students scored very near the cut-off score. Students scoring below 77 may be viewed as students in need of interventions and further assessments. The fewer words read, the more the student might need more intense interventions such as those in Tier 2 or 3.

As educators establish a process for determining which students at their school should receive Tier 1, 2, or 3 services, they face challenges associated with selecting criteria for tiers. Research-based criteria of risk, like those provided by the *DIBELS* for reading, are also available for behavioral issues; schools can look at office discipline referrals, for example, through School-Wide Information System (www.swis.org). These recommended criteria can be useful to schools in determining whether students should receive Tier 1, 2, or 3 services. However, according to Ervin (n.d.):

> Unfortunately, research-based risk criteria are not always available for other important targets, meaning that educators need to consider how they will decide to match tiered services to student needs. When research-based risk criteria or expected levels of performance are unavailable, educators must select standards for comparison (e.g., professional experience, teacher expectations, parental expectations, developmental norms, medical standards, curriculum standards, national norms, local norms, and classroom peer performance), and this is not an easy task. Furthermore, even when research-based risk criteria are available, schools serving high numbers of students at risk for reading and or behavioral problems may not have sufficient resources to provide Tier 3 interventions to all students who fall into risk categories.

Ideally, RTI models are developed so that students can not only move into more intense levels after undergoing interventions at the previous level, but also that those who need more intensive levels from the beginning can be "triaged" directly into those levels. Tier 3 services are designed to address the needs of students who are experiencing significant problems and/or unresponsive to Tier 1 and Tier 2 efforts. Schools should establish guidelines for determining how students will enter into Tier 1, 2, or 3 levels of support. Although guidelines may vary from school to school, students in need of Tier 3 services should be able to access these services in one of two ways. First, students receiving Tier 1 or Tier 2 supports who are not making adequate progress and are unresponsive to the continuum of supports available at Tier 1 or Tier 2 might be moved into Tier 3 to receive more intensive intervention supports. Second, there should be a mechanism through which students who are experiencing very severe or significant academic, behavioral, or socioemotional problems can be sent directly into Tier 3 to receive necessary intensive and individualized intervention supports. For some students, the second option is necessary to receive needed supports in a timely fashion. Thus, in contrast to a fixed, multigating system wherein students would only be able to receive more intensive services (Tier 3) following some period of less intensive services (Tier 1 or 2), the RTI approach should allow some flexibility to serve students based on their level of need in a timely and efficient manner.

Progress Monitoring

According to Fuchs, Vaughn, and Fuchs (in press), progress monitoring plays four critical roles within a multilevel prevention system: (1) evaluating primary prevention, (2) identifying adequate response to intervention, (3) designing individualized interventions for Tier 3, and (4) determining when to discontinue Tier 3 interventions.

First, progress monitoring helps us determine whether primary prevention (the core instructional program at Tier 1) is working for each student and for all students in the aggregate. Remember, typically 15 percent of the students in a given classroom will be in need of Tier 2 interventions and perhaps as many as 5 percent will need interventions at Tier 3. When percentages at these tiers are larger than expected, and/or include disproportionate numbers of children from poverty or nondominant cultures, schools should re-examine how they test and teach these students at Tier 1.

Decisions should not be based on a single measurement. Fuchs, Vaughn, and Fuchs (in press) warn against using a one-time measure such as a state test to determine who is at risk: "There is a danger in using one-time screening in that it may indicate falsely that the student needs secondary intervention when the student might have learned to read or perform the mathematics process without interventions." In a first-grade RTI experiment (Fuchs, Compton, Fuchs, Bryant, & Davis, in press), 50 percent of the control group designated as at risk on one of these one-time fall assessments were not given interventions. Yet by January, these students all read and tested normally. Schools need to avoid these false positives not only because they are expensive, but also because they falsely label the students. Because screenings, especially at kindergarten and first grade, typically identify many false alarms, Fuchs, Compton, Fuchs, Bryant, and Davis (in press) recommend that one-time screening should constitute only the first step in designating risk and that screening be supplemented with progress monitoring. Students who are suspected to be at risk based on screening should be followed with five to eight weeks of progress monitoring to determine their response at Tier 1 (Compton, Fuchs, Fuchs, & Bryant, 2006).

Progress monitoring also helps us distinguish adequate from inadequate response to the secondary prevention and thereby identify students who may have a learning disability. Decisions to continue the intervention, change the intervention, fade the intervention, move the student back to Tier 1, or move the student to Tier 3 are all made on the strength of the progress monitoring.

Finally, progress monitoring helps us to design the more individualized interventions for Tier 3 by making clear what has not worked in the past. Progress monitoring is used to inductively formulate an effective, individualized instructional program.

The goal is to return the student to a less intensive level of the multilevel prevention system as soon as possible, while continuing to monitor his or her progress in case a need re-emerges for intensive intervention at Tier 3. As we monitor how a student responds to intervention at Tier 3, we can then determine when a return to Tier 2 or even Tier 1 is possible.

Frequency of Monitoring

In the literature, we often see recommendations for weekly assessment to determine if a child at Tier 2 is making adequate progress using the prescribed interventions. In effective reading interventions, however, students are often more frequently assessed to measure their reading growth. Typically, students will read for one to two minutes while the teacher calculates how many words per minute they are reading (Fuchs, Fuchs, Hosp, & Jenkins, 2001; Hasbrouck & Tindal, 2006). These results can be graphed so that teachers, other educators, parents, and the students themselves can identify their progress. (See Denton & Mathes, 2003; Fletcher, Denton, Fuchs, & Vaughn, 2005; Vaughn et al., 2006).

Bender and Shores (2007) say that Tier 2 assessments—either formative or summative—should be conducted on a daily basis. They further state that students at Tier 2 can be better served with the observations of other educators outside the students' regular classroom teacher. Their argument for the importance of the decision-making process at this level is viable. After all, we are considering, ultimately, whether a child is learning disabled and how best to serve his or her needs. The outcome will affect the child for a long time to come.

Now that we've discussed decision making and progress monitoring, let's examine some intervention strategies in the key areas of reading and math.

Reading Interventions

In 2000, the National Reading Panel (2000) conducted a comprehensive analysis of existing reading research that met high standards for quality. The conclusions of that study show that good reading instruction addresses the domains of phonemic awareness, phonics, fluency, vocabulary, and comprehension. These are also crucial areas for intervention.

Phonemic Awareness, Phonics, and Fluency

In her article about supporting struggling readers, Carolyn Denton (2010) discusses a landmark report from the National Research Council:

> The final report, called *Preventing Reading Difficulties in Young Children* (Snow, Burns, and Griffin, 1998) concludes that most reading problems can be prevented by providing effective instruction and intervention in preschool and in the primary grades. The NRC noted that for students to learn to read well they must (a) understand how sounds are represented by print and be able to apply this understanding to read and spell words, (b) practice reading enough to become fluent readers, (c) learn new vocabulary words, and (d) learn to self-monitor when reading to make sure what they read makes sense and to correct their own errors. The NRC also found that it was important that teachers provide explicit instruction in phonemic awareness and phonics integrated with many opportunities to read and write meaningful, connected text. (They purposely used the word *integrated* rather than *balanced*. It isn't enough simply to add on components of a fragmented curriculum to balance one with another.) Finally, they noted that effective reading teachers adapt their instruction, making changes designed to meet the needs of different students.

In kindergarten and first grade (and for older students who need it), reading instruction should include teaching phonics and phonemic awareness or word study explicitly. According to Sousa (2005), students who have phonemic awareness can:

1. Recognize words beginning with the same sound,

2. isolate and say the first and last sounds in a word,

3. combine and blend sounds in a word, and

4. break a word into its separate sounds. (p. 34)

Students sent to Tiers 2 or 3 should be assessed to determine if part or all of phonemic awareness is keeping them from reading. These skills can be and should be directly taught. As a matter of fact, according to Shaywitz (2003), phonemic awareness and letter knowledge are the two best predictors of how well students will learn to read. Students in middle school and high school who struggle with reading need emphasis on these two skills.

Sousa (2005) offers the following directions for teaching phonemic awareness:

1. Assess early to determine student needs.

2. Utilize the suggestions of Yopp and Yopp (2000) for a complete phonemic awareness program that includes matching, isolating, substituting, blending, segmenting, and deleting sounds in words.

3. Limit the number of phoneme manipulation techniques to two or less at a time.

4. Directly teach students how to manipulate phonemes along with letters.

5. Use small groups for teaching phonemic awareness.

6. In preschool, focus on developing an awareness of rhyme and in separating words into syllables and then syllables into phonemes.

7. In kindergarten, focus on practicing the sound structure of the words, the recognition and production of letters, and teaching print concepts.

8. In grade 1, provide students with explicit instruction and practice with sound structures that lead to phonemic awareness. Make students aware of the sound–spelling correspondences and spelling conventions in written words, teach sight recognition of frequently used words, and provide time for independent reading.

In addition to phonics, we talk a great deal in education about reading fluency. Lack of fluency often lies at the heart of reading problems. Sousa (2005, p. 82) defines fluency as "the ability to read a text orally with speed, accuracy, and proper expression." Students who are fluent can do those things and know what they have read. Struggling students may take so much time trying to decode words that they do not know that they wind up reading a sentence but have no idea what they read. As students get older and the sentences get longer, this becomes more and more of a problem. The problem has to do with how the brain takes in and processes information. New information comes to us through the senses (hearing, seeing, smelling, tasting, and touching), after which the brain makes a quick decision as to whether it will do anything with the information or simply toss it out (Tileston, 2005). The information that is not discarded is first stored in immediate memory, then sent to working memory, where it may reside for minutes to days. It is in working memory that conscious processing takes place. In the act of reading sentences, Sousa (2005) explains, "the visual and memory systems of the brain must decode and then retain the words at the beginning of a sentence for a period of time while the reader's eyes move to the end of the sentence" (p. 48). As a result, when the sentence structure becomes longer and more complex, struggling readers will have difficulty remembering what they read at the beginning of the sentence by the time they get to the end. Thus, students may read a sentence but not comprehend its meaning. According to Sousa (2005, p. 49),

> A child's ability to store words temporarily in working memory depends on several factors, such as age, experience, and language proficiency. But the code that readers of any age use to store written words and phrases is a phonological code. Consequently, phonological coding skills are crucial for using and developing the ability of working memory to store representations of written words.)

Vocabulary and Comprehension

We have already discussed extensively the importance of vocabulary to Tier 1 instruction, particularly for children from poverty and minority cultures. It is woven throughout all reading strategies, together with comprehension. Teachers can build vocabulary and comprehension by: chunking content; using prior knowledge; encouraging reading; teaching essential skills and strategies; providing explicit, systematic instruction with lots of practice and feedback; and providing opportunities to apply skills and strategies in reading and writing meaningful text, with teacher support. These things can and should be done at Tier 1, and they become even more critical in Tier 2 and Tier 3 when delivering proven, research-based interventions in reading.

Chunking content

Chunking or creating gists is a method of breaking down sentences (at the youngest level) or breaking down chapters (at the highest level) to help readers make meaning of what they've read, be it a sentence or a whole book.

For example, in the sentence "The man in the yellow taxi swerved to miss the red bus stopped at the corner," students who are struggling with words such as *swerved, stopped,* and *corner* may be able to read each word but not be able to tell you what the sentence means. To help them, we might chunk the sentence into clauses, starting with "the man in the yellow taxi swerved" and helping students build a mental model of a yellow taxi swerving. Next, we could take the clause "swerved to miss the red bus stopped at the corner" and again build mental models and correctly identify words that are not known.

Sousa (2005) says that to chunk for readers at the beginning level, we want to break down sentences to the individual clauses that make up the sentence so that students use working memory to help them comprehend the sentence (clause 1 + clause 2 + clause 3 = sentence 1 gist). For students who can understand what they read in a sentence but not in a paragraph, we chunk the sentences (sentence gist 1 + sentence gist 2 + sentence gist 3 = paragraph 1 gist). At the third level, we would do the same thing with paragraphs so that we get the gist of a chapter. And finally, at level four, students would take the gist of each chapter to understand the gist of the entire book.

Using prior knowledge

Prior knowledge helps us to create mental models for understanding. Find out the prior knowledge of your students so that you can better understand the reasons for comprehension difficulties. A child from Mexico may not have any background knowledge to help her understand passages about George Washington, for example.

I sometimes do a demonstration lesson on immigration to demonstrate this concept. In a school where the children are middle class and have lived in the United States all their lives, I would not expect them to understand why people would leave most of their possessions behind, get into a small boat, and risk their lives to go to a place where they know no one. To create background knowledge where it does not exist, I have to help students to think in a different way. I ask, "What would have to happen in this country for you to pick up what you could in your arms and set out under dangerous circumstances to go to a place to start over?" Next, I chunk their answers into categories—the same categories that we will use when we discuss immigration. I ask, "What would have to happen in this country politically? Medically? In the religious realm?" I have about seven categories that I use to make this point. I have set up the categories that we will discuss throughout the unit on why people immigrate so that my students can build empathy for people who do immigrate to this country. A similar lesson uses the wonderful book *Should Bugs Bug You* by Zaner-Bloser (2003), which begins by asking readers to create three categories: insects that are pests, insects that are helpful, and insects that can be both pests and helpful. Students make predictions based on their past experience with bugs. Later in the unit, after the students have read about insects, they mindmap which are helpful to man and which are bothersome. Again, we are creating background knowledge before reading.

Encouraging reading

Look at the choices in your classroom and in your school. Do the choices reflect the interests of your students? Their ethnicity? Their gender? Kunjufu (2005) talks about visiting schools that say they do not see color and that they treat all students the same. Yet when he visits their classrooms, the bulletin boards, the books, and the lesson plans do not reflect the color of their students. If we want African American males to read, we must provide reading materials that appeal to them.

I grew up in poverty, and yet I have not only a love of reading, but also a love of the arts. We often think of the arts as something for the rich. My school thought children from poverty should have enriched experiences, so the school rule was that prior to fifth grade, all students would be taken to the symphony, the ballet, and the opera. And they wouldn't just go—they would go knowing what was going on, the purpose of the music, the instruments that made the music, and the background of the opera or ballet. We need to do the same with reading for children from poverty. Reading should be a reward in the classroom, and it should incorporate the interests of the students.

Teaching essential skills and strategies

Effective reading teachers teach skills and strategies, as well as concepts. Skills are things students learn to do. In reading, students must learn skills such as associating letters with their sounds and blending sounds to form words. Strategies are routines or plans of actions that can be used to accomplish a goal or work through difficulty. Students can be taught strategies to use when they come to a word they don't know, strategies for spelling unknown words, strategies to help them write summaries of paragraphs, and other kinds of strategies.

A critical part of effective reading instruction is explicitly teaching students what to do when they get to a hard word. In one research-validated early reading intervention program, young students are taught to use a three-part strategy when they try to read difficult words: "Look for parts you know, sound it out, and check it" (Denton & Hocker, 2006, p. 144). The steps are as follows:

1. Look for parts of the word you know. In the earliest stages of learning to read, students may find a letter or a letter combination (such as *th* or *ing*) that they know. Later, they may recognize common word endings (such as *-ot* in *pot*, *rot*, or *cot*). Still later, they may identify roots or base words, such as the root *-spect* (which means to see) in the words *inspect* and *spectacles*, or common prefixes and suffixes like *pre-* or *-ly*.

2. Sound it out. Students should be taught from the earliest lessons to use a sounding-out strategy to read unfamiliar words. They should learn how to blend sounds and larger word parts together to read words and how to apply this strategy when reading real text. Some teachers in kindergarten or first grade teach students to identify unknown words by looking at pictures on the page or by identifying one or two letters of the word, but they're teaching their students to use the problematic guessing strategy described by the middle school student in the scenario.

3. Check it. Denton and Hocker (2006) describe this step as follows:

> After students sound out the unfamiliar word, the last step of the three-part word reading strategy is to teach students to put the newly solved word back into the sentence and to check it to be sure it makes sense. Thus, the meaning of the word in context is not ignored; it is used as the checking mechanism. Studies of skilled young readers show that this is the main way they use context—not for guessing what words are, but for checking to be sure that their reading is making sense so they can make corrections when it doesn't make sense. (p. 144)

Provide ample time for students to understand through mental models, and teach skills so that they become automatic. Make sure that students have the prerequisite content knowledge as well, such as the vocabulary expected for the grade level and subject area. National, state, and local standards provide that information for you. English learners and students from poverty may not have been exposed to all of the words in the standards, and consequently we might think that they need interventions at Tier 2 or Tier 3 when what they need is to learn the vocabulary. Provide many opportunities for students at all tiers and especially those at Tiers 2 and 3 to "play" with vocabulary. Use visual tools such as graphic organizers to allow students to further their knowledge of the vocabulary beyond its meaning.

Providing explicit, systematic instruction with lots of practice and feedback

According to Denton (2010), "Students with learning difficulties benefit from explicit instruction in decoding skills and strategies, fluency (modeling fluent reading, directly teaching how to interpret punctuation marks when reading orally, etc.), vocabulary word meanings and word-learning strategies, and comprehension strategies." When a teacher provides explicit instruction, she or he clearly models or demonstrates skills and strategies and provides clear descriptions of new concepts (providing both clear examples and nonexamples). Students don't have to infer what they are supposed to learn. For example, a teacher who is explicitly teaching first-grade students to sound out words demonstrates this process step by step, then provides opportunities for students to practice the skill with the teacher's feedback and support. If a student is not successful, the teacher models again. The teacher may have students sound out a few words along with him or her. Eventually, the students apply the skill independently to sound out simple words. Students who are easily confused are more likely to be successful when teachers demonstrate and clearly explain what they need to learn. On the other hand, if confusions are not addressed and foundational skills are not mastered, it is likely that students will become more and more confused, resulting in serious reading problems.

Systematic instruction is carefully sequenced so that easier skills are taught before more difficult skills. Letter-sound correspondences and phonics skills (such as sounding out words or applying the "silent *e*" rule) are taught in a predetermined order with a clear scope and sequence so that no gaps in students' learning result. The pace of introduction of new material is reasonable to allow struggling learners to master key skills, and much of each lesson consists of practice of previously introduced skills, strategies, and concepts and the integration of these with the newly taught material. Students' learning is monitored, so that teachers can reteach key skills when needed.

Struggling readers also need a lot of practice, with and without teacher support, as well as ongoing feedback. Published reading programs rarely include enough practice activities for at-risk readers to master skills and strategies. Students with learning difficulties typically need extended guided, independent, and cumulative practice. During guided practice, students practice with teacher feedback. Students need both positive and corrective feedback. Specific positive feedback calls attention to behaviors and processes the student is implementing well. Students also need to know when they made mistakes. If clear corrective feedback is not provided, students are likely to continue to make the same errors, in effect "practicing their mistakes" (Denton & Hocker, 2006, p. 17) and forming bad habits that are difficult to break. Students also need independent practice, during which they implement skills and strategies without teacher support (but with close teacher monitoring, and with reteaching when necessary). Finally, students at risk for reading difficulties need large amounts of cumulative practice over time to learn to apply skills and strategies automatically when they read, just as skilled readers do. Cumulative practice means practicing newly learned items mixed in with items learned earlier, so that skills are not taught and "dropped." Students with reading problems often need a lot of review. One effective way to provide extra practice opportunities in the reading classroom is the implementation of peer tutoring routines in which students are paired and taught how to work together to practice skills they have been taught (see Fuchs & Fuchs, 2005; McMaster, Fuchs, & Fuchs, 2006; Saenz, Fuchs, & Fuchs, 2005). There is also preliminary evidence indicating that practice in phonics and word identification may be more effective for first-grade at-risk readers if it includes hands-on manipulation of items such as magnetic letters or word cards (Pullen, Lane, Lloyd, Nowak, & Ryals, 2005).

Providing opportunities to apply skills and strategies in reading and writing meaningful text with teacher support

Clearly, it isn't enough for students to learn to read or spell lists of words. The real purpose of reading is to get meaning from text, and the purpose of writing is to convey meaning with text. It is very important that students have the opportunity to apply word identification and spelling skills as they read and write connected text. This process must be supported by teachers who model for students how to apply what they have learned and give students feedback about their reading and writing. For example, students must be taught what to do when they get to a hard word. The most common characteristic of poor readers of all ages is the tendency to guess words that are difficult, sometimes using just a few letters. Often students make random guesses that don't make sense—and then simply continue reading, apparently unaware of their error. This quote from a middle school student, taken from a moving article about students in middle school with severe reading problems, describes the situation well:

> Sometimes when students in my class read, they might know how to say simple words okay, but they will skip over the big words. They look around to see if anyone is even listening to them. But they don't fix them; they just keep going. They stumble over words, trying to sound them out. Sometimes they don't even know they made a mistake, and when they figure out the words, they don't have a clue what it all means. They just keep going. (McCray, Vaughn, & Neal, 2001, p. 22)

As this student observed, it is nearly impossible for students to understand what they are reading—to get meaning from text—when they can't read the words on the page accurately and fluently. Students need explicit instruction, modeling, and practice in vocabulary and reading comprehension, but many students with reading problems continue to need instruction in phonics and word study even when they are in the upper elementary and secondary grades (Fletcher, 2007).

Mathematics Interventions

Any mathematics intervention should incorporate five instructional principles: (1) instructional explicitness, (2) instructional design that eases the learning challenge, (3) a strong conceptual basis for procedures that are taught, (4) cumulative review as part of drill and practice, and (5) motivators to help students regulate their attention and behavior (Fuchs, Vaughn, & Fuchs, in press). Let's look at how they might be implemented in a three-tier model.

Instructional Explicitness

Most students in a given math class are taught using a collectivist approach. Students who struggle with math, however, need very explicit mathematics instruction. Fuchs, Vaughn, and Fuchs (in press) cite a meta-analysis of 58 math studies by Kroesbergen and van Luit (2003) that shows students with math disabilities learn best when the instruction is explicit rather than discovery oriented. Explicit instruction has a high effect size on student learning, in other words. It is important to point out here that explicit instruction is *not* lecture.

Instructional Design That Eases the Learning Challenge

Effective instructional design provides the necessary scaffolding to help students understand how the math works and to keep up with the math principles learned. That is:

> The goal is to anticipate and eliminate misunderstandings by means of precise explanations and with the use of carefully sequenced and integrated instruction. The purpose is to close the achievement gap as quickly as possible. This may be especially important for mathematics, which involves many branches and strands that may be distinct, each with its own conceptual and procedural demands. So, given the ever changing and multiple demands of the mathematics curriculum, instructional efficiency is critical, creating the need for the tutor or the program on which the tutor relies to minimize the learning challenges for the student. (Fuchs, Vaughn, & Fuchs, in press)

Advance organizers can be helpful to students as they try to keep the various principles learned in an order that helps them review and reuse the mathematics learned. Figure 5.2 (page 126) is an example of an organizer that can be given to students to help them clarify what they have learned.

Math Principle	Example	Vocabulary to Know	Notes to Remember	Mistakes to Avoid
Simplify each side of an equation.	$5x = 3(4 + 1)$ $4 + 1 = 5$ $5x = 3(5)$ $5x = 15$	*Equation*: An equation is a mathematical sentence with an equal (=) sign in it. Examples: $3 + 5 = 8$ $3x + 1 = 4$ Nonexample: $2x + 7x + 1$ The nonexample does not have an = sign in it. *Variable*: A variable is a letter that is used to represent a number. Some equations have variables in them, and some do not. Example: $3x = 9$ Nonexample $3(3) = 9$	Add what is inside the ( ). Substitute 5 for $4 + 1$ Multiply: $3(5)$.	Whatever is on the left side of the = sign stays on the left side. Whatever is on the right side of the = sign stays on the right side.

Figure 5.2: An advance organizer for math.

Because mathematics has its own vocabulary, I have included a place for important vocabulary words involved in the math skill. I've also included a place for the students' own notes. While this organizer may seem redundant or unnecessary to mathematicians, it is of great value to students who struggle with this week's math lesson, not to mention trying to remember the math from two weeks ago. The same kind of chart can be used in reading to keep track of stories, poems and books read, their main characters, and so on. It is a great review tool and a good way to reinforce the learning by comparing the lessons to one another. Students today tend to be visual and kinesthetic; they are used to interacting with the world around them. We need to provide opportunities for them to develop visual models of how math works and to give them the tools to help them to be successful. Visual tools such as organizers have a high effect size on student learning in both mathematics and in reading.

Another advance organizer that is helpful to struggling students is to provide students with heuristics or algorithms in advance of learning skills so that they can check their own work. Heuristics are general rules that apply to a skill when we do not expect to get the same answer or product each time. For example, suppose students are going to create mindmaps of the types of shapes to be learned in their second-grade classroom. They are given a list of the shapes that they will be studying and are given general rules for creating mindmaps such as those in figure 5.3 (page 128).

While the mindmaps will have similarities, the teacher will not expect (or desire) the mindmaps to all look alike. The teacher has provided general guidelines in writing (and has shown examples and nonexamples to the students), but the guidelines are not so rigid as to get the same results every time.

However, in mathematics, when problem solving, we usually want a specific answer, and variations will not be correct. When we want the answer or finished product to always be the same, we provide algorithms, which are the specific steps that must be followed to get the right answer. An example for all students might look like the example in figure 5.4 (page 128) from Long (2006).

We will be creating mindmaps of the following shapes:

Square

Triangle

Sphere

Circle

Cone

Rectangle

Your mindmap will show your topic in the center: Shapes

Your mindmap will use different colors for each of its spokes and shapes.

Your mindmap will contain both words and pictures.

Spell your words correctly.

Write your words neatly.

Figure 5.3: Sample mindmap heuristics.

There are three steps to solving an equation with one variable.

Step 1: Simplify each side of the equation.

Step 2: Add and/or subtract.

Step 3: Multiply or divide.

Figure 5.4: Sample algorithm for solving equations.

For students at Tier 2 or 3, an advance organizer should be much more detailed. It might include, for example, notes on when to use the order of operations or the distributive property, examples of what each step looks like, and rationale for why it's important to do certain steps in a particular order or fashion. Advance organizers provide students with specific rules so that when the answer is not correct, they can check to see if they followed each step correctly. The goal is to teach the foundational skills for solving equations while providing scaffolding through the organizers to help students evaluate their own work and solve equations independently.

A Strong Conceptual Basis for Procedures That Are Taught

Procedural knowledge is difficult; students must have ample opportunity to practice skills, whether in mathematics or reading, so that they can achieve *automaticity*. Automaticity means the student can perform the skill automatically, without having to think it through each time. For example, when you first learned to drive a car, you thought about getting everything just right when you first got in and about the steps to driving (gears and so on), but with practice, you were able to drive a car without having to think about each step. Similarly, effective teachers provide guided practice first and then additional practice over time until students show automaticity when problem solving or reading words.

Cumulative Review as Part of Drill and Practice

Using effective drill and practice includes providing practice in sorting problems into types, mixing problem types within the daily lesson (once at least two problem types have been introduced), and daily review. Fuchs et al. (in press) say:

> Instruction purposefully conceptualizes, organizes and teaches students to recognize problem types that pertain broadly to the kinds of problems found in the general education curriculum in high stakes tests. That way,

novel word problems are not random events for students, each of which requires the creation of a solution strategy. Rather, the student recognizes novel problems as familiar, using schemas for problem types that the program teaches, and thereby deciphers when to apply which set of solution rules he or she has learned. Finally, instruction conceptualizes transfer within the same problem-type structure, so that irrelevant information, finding missing information in any of the three slots of an equation, and finding relevant information within charts or graphs recurs predictably and efficiently across problem-type instructional units.

This is reflected in continual reliance on the foundational skills taught in the introductory unit and the use of mixed problems types within conceptual instruction, sorting practice, and paper-and-pencil review.

Motivators to Help Students Regulate Their Attention and Behavior and to Work Hard

Students at risk for poor academic outcomes often display attention, motivation, and self-regulation difficulties that may adversely affect their behavior and learning (Fuchs, Fuchs, & Maxwell, 2006; Montague, 2007). By the time students enter secondary intervention, they often have experienced at least some failure, which may cause some to avoid the emotional stress associated with mathematics. They no longer try to learn for fear of failing. For this reason, secondary intervention must incorporate systematic self-regulation and motivators, and for many students, tangible reinforcers are required. The best way to reinforce the drive to learn is by helping students to experience success—not by watering down material, but by adding scaffolding so that they can be independently successful.

A Final Note on Tier 3

Tier 3 intervention differs from secondary intervention because it is more intensive, carried out in very small groups or individually, and pinpoints very specific skill deficits. Tier 3 interventions come after students have shown that they are not making adequate progress either in the general education classroom at Tier 1 or with validated reading or math programs in Tier 2. For these students, very specific programs tailored to their individual gaps in learning must be used. Careful monitoring will also take place to determine whether these students will respond to the more intense interventions. According to Fuchs, Vaughn, and Fuchs (in press), "For designing instructional programs that are individually tailored, two approaches are generally used: deductive and inductive approaches." The deductive approach "involves administering a battery of cognitive assessments to determine strengths and weaknesses and then designing a program to take advantage of strengths and to make up for weaknesses. Unfortunately, a deductive approach has proven difficult to design and has been shown to be largely ineffective," they conclude. The inductive approach, on the other hand, "relies strongly on progress monitoring. That is, an initial instructional program, based on information collected in secondary prevention is implemented" (Fuchs, Vaughn, & Fuchs, in press). Once the interventions needed have been determined, the teacher or tutor monitors the progress of the student at least weekly. By monitoring frequently, decisions can be made about whether to change the intervention, continue it, or gradually fade it:

> As the teacher conducts revisions to the program, ongoing progress monitoring continues, and the resulting data provide the teacher with information about which revisions accelerate student learning (and therefore should be retained and enhanced) and which program elements fail to enhance student learning (and therefore should be removed from the program). In this way, the teacher deductively designs an individualized program. (Fuchs, Vaughn, & Fuchs, in press)

It is important to note that even when students are making progress and a decision to move them back to Tier 2 interventions takes place, progress monitoring takes place so that the Tier 3 interventions can be reinitiated if needed. The goal, of course, is to eventually be able to place the child successfully back into the general instructional program.

In Conclusion

Students receive interventions at Tier 2 or Tier 3 when their assessments and subsequent interventions demonstrate that they need additional or more intensive forms of interventions in order to be successful. Assessment results will often indicate that steps in either learning mathematics skills or reading skills have been omitted or simply not understood. In this chapter, I have provided some principles to guide educators as they make critical decisions. Students at Tiers 2 and 3 should be served in very small groups or individually so that the gaps can be pinpointed exactly and so that instruction is individualized. Progress monitoring is critical, as is documentation for decisions that have a lasting effect on the child. Our goal is to fill in the gaps and to be able to gradually fade the interventions so that the student can fully function and be successful in the general education classroom with a research-based curriculum and highly qualified teacher.

Learning Log

In this chapter	Your thoughts
How will you make the decision to move a student to Tier 2? To Tier 3? Do you have a process in place to directly move a student to Tier 3 if the gap is severe?	

Epilogue

Throughout this book, I have provided guidelines to help prevent errors that are made due to teachers not knowing the cultural differences of students, particularly in regard to learning. In determining interventions, we must take into account the culture of the student first. Is the impoverished minority student performing at a lower level because of the cultural differences in how she learns, how she views education, her learning modality, her lack of vocabulary, or a genuine learning disability?

The goal of any RTI model should be to increase student achievement. That said, rather than focusing only on percentages or numbers of identified students, schools and individual teachers should focus on outcomes. A school might have a disproportionate number of Hispanic students receiving special education services aimed at increasing their reading comprehension. Effectiveness measures must relate to learning outcomes. Are these students making progress at a rate consistent with other students, and is there an exit plan? If the answers are no, then why? Further analysis may be required. For example, is the implementation plan adequate, and does it include modifications for culture and language differences?

We have not closed the achievement gaps because we keep getting the diagnosis wrong and, thus, the interventions do not match up. This is our opportunity to get it right. To make a significant difference in learning for children, teachers need to modify, or differentiate, effective instructional practices in order to improve academic achievement *and* to close the gap in achievement for students from poverty, students of diverse cultures, and English learners. Response to intervention holds great promise if we join together to make sure that we use evidence-based decisions to determine the real gaps and apply culturally differentiated best practices to close them.

Glossary

culture. The social groups with which individuals identify and that create group values, expectations, and goals.

curriculum-based assessment (CBA). A measurement that uses direct observation and recording of a student's performance on the local curriculum as a basis for gathering information to make instructional decisions. All assessments used under progress monitoring that meet the following three criteria:

1. The measurement materials have been aligned with the school curriculum.

2. The measurement is given frequently.

3. The data from the measurement are used for making decisions on instruction.

curriculum-based management (CBM). A form of CBA that uses standardized assessments to sample the year-long curriculum in exactly the same way each time, rather than teacher-designed assessments to measure learning objectives that change over time.

early intervening services (EIS). The preventive components of No Child Left Behind and the Individuals with Disabilities Education Improvement Act of 2004.

fidelity of implementation. Implementation of an intervention, program, or curriculum in accordance with research findings or developers' specifications.

functional assessment. A measure that includes a process to identify problems, to determine the function or purpose of behaviors, and to develop interventions that teach acceptable alternatives to behaviors.

IDEIA. The Individuals with Disabilities Education Improvement Act of 2004, also referred to as IDEA 2004. The original law was passed in 1975; the latest reauthorization occurred in 2004. This federal statute addresses public education and services for students with disabilities ages three through twenty-one.

learning disability (LD). *See* **specific learning disability.**

poverty. Lack of access to goods and services severe enough to create hardship, illness, or hunger.

problem-solving approach to RTI. An approach that assumes that no given intervention will be effective for all students. This approach generally has four stages (problem identification, problem analysis, plan implementation, and plan evaluation), is sensitive to individual student differences, and depends on the fidelity of implementing interventions.

problem-solving team. The team that develops academic and behavior intervention strategies, oversees assessment to determine student progress, and analyzes data to determine if the instructional strategies need to be faded, changed, or continued. The team is usually made up of both general education teachers and teachers in special programs. Possible team members include a coordinator or curriculum specialist, a consultant or specialist in RTI, the child's parent, the principal, classroom teachers, and others with expertise in data analysis and interventions (academic and behavioral).

progress monitoring. A scientifically based practice used to assess students' academic performance and evaluate the effectiveness of instruction. Progress monitoring can be implemented with individual students or entire classes. The process also is used to monitor implementation of specific interventions.

response to intervention. The practice of providing high-quality instruction and interventions matched to students' needs, monitoring progress frequently to make changes in instruction or goals, and applying student-response data to important educational decisions.

scientifically based research. Education-related research that meets the following criteria:

- Analyzes and gauges the effect of teaching on students' achievement

- Studies large numbers of students

- Includes experimental and control groups

- Applies a rigorous peer-review process

- Includes replication studies to validate results

specific learning disability (SLD). The legal description for a learning disability that meets the criteria described in IDEA 2004 regarding critical areas of proficiency, benchmarks of achievement and progress, quality of instruction and intervention, processes for monitoring progress, and more. (See IDEA Partnership, n.d., for the full criteria.)

standard protocol intervention. Use of the same empirically validated interventions for all students with similar academic or behavioral needs; facilitates quality control; the alternative to the problem-solving approach.

tiered model. A common model of most often three tiers that delineate levels of instructional interventions based on students' learning needs.

universal screening. A process of reviewing student performance through formal or informal assessment measures to determine progress in relation to benchmarks directly related to learning standards.

validated intervention. An instructional practice that appears in professional journals and is shown to improve student learning when used correctly in the classroom.

References and Resources

American Psychiatric Association. (2000). *Diagnostic and statistical manual of mental disorders (DSM-IV-TR)*. Washington, DC: Author.

Armbruster, B. (1996). Schema theory and the design of context-area textbooks. *Educational Psychologist, 21*, 253–276.

Arroyo, C. (2008, January). *The funding gap 2007.* Washington, DC: Education Trust.

Barakat, H. I. (1993). *The Arab world: Society, culture, and state.* Berkeley: University of California Press.

Bender, W. N., & Shores, C. (2007). *Response to intervention: A practical guide for every teacher [Facilitator's guide to multimedia kit].* Thousand Oaks, CA: Corwin Press.

Blake, I. K. (1994). Language development and socialization in young African-American children. In P. M. Greenfield and R. R Cocking (Eds.), *Cross-cultural roots of minority child development* (pp. 167–195). Hillsdale, NJ: Lawrence Erlbaum Associates.

Brown v. Board of Education, 347 U.S. 483 (1954).

Brown-Chidsey, R. B., & Steege, M. W. (2005). *Response to intervention: Principles and methods for effective practice.* New York: Guilford Press.

Chinn, P. C., & Hughes, S. (1987). Representation of minority students in special education classes. *Remedial and Special Education, 8*(4), 41–46.

Clauss-Ehlers, C. S. (2006). *Diversity training for classroom teaching: A manual for students and educators.* New York: Springer.

Clotfelter, C. T., Ladd, H. F., & Vigdor, J. L. (2007). *How and why do teacher credentials matter for student achievement?* Accessed at www.caldercenter.org/PDF/1001058_Teacher_Credentials .pdf on August 14, 2009.

Cohen, D. K., & Ball, D. L. (2001, September). Making change: Instruction and its improvement. *Phi Delta Kappan, 83*(1), 73–77.

Compton, D. L., Fuchs, D., Fuchs, L. S., & Bryant, J. D. (2006). Selecting at-risk readers in first grade for early intervention: A two-year longitudinal study of decision rules and procedures. *Journal of Educational Psychology, 98*(2), 394–409.

Cozzens, L. (1995). *Brown v. Board of Education.* Accessed at www .watson.org/~lisa/blackhistory/early-civilrights/brown.html on February 15, 2008.

Daly, A. J., & Chrispeels, J. (2005). From problem to possibility: Leadership for implementing and deepening Effective Schools processes. *Journal for Effective Schools, 4*(1), 7–25.

Delgado Gaitan, C. (1993). Research and policy in reconceptualizing family-school relationships. In P. Phelan & A. Davidson (Eds.), *Cultural diversity and educational policy and change* (pp. 139–159). New York: Teachers College Press.

Delgado Gaitan, C. (1994). Socializing young children in Mexican-American families: An intergenerational perspective. In P. M. Greenfield and R. R. Cocking (Eds.), *Cross-cultural roots of minority child development* (pp. 55–86). Hillsdale, NJ: Lawrence Erlbaum Associates.

Denton, C. A. (2010). *Classroom reading instruction that supports struggling readers: Key components for effective teaching.* Accessed at www.rtinetwork.org/essential/tieredinstruction/tier1/ effectiveteaching on June 28, 2010.

Denton, C. A., & Hocker, J. L. (2006). *Responsive reading instruction: Flexible intervention for struggling readers in the early grades.* Longmont, CO: Sopris West.

Denton, C. A., & Mathes, P. G. (2003). Intervention for struggling readers: Possibilities and challenges. In B. R. Foorman (Ed.), *Preventing and remediating reading difficulties: Bringing science to scale* (pp. 229–251). Timonium, MD: York Press.

Doidge, N. (2007). *The brain that changes itself: Stories of personal triumph from the frontiers of brain science.* New York: Viking.

Donovan, M. S., & Cross, C. T. (Eds.). (2002). *Minority students in special and gifted education.* Washington, DC: National Academies Press.

Education for All Handicapped Children Act of 1975, Pub. L. No. 94-142.

Education Trust. (2005, Winter). *The funding gap 2005: Low-income and minority students shortchanged by most states.* Washington, DC: Author.

Education Trust. (2008). *Their fair share: How Texas-sized gaps in teacher quality shortchange poor and minority students.* Washington, DC: Author.

Elementary and Secondary Education Act of 1965, Pub. L. No. 89-10.

Ervin, R. A. (n.d.). Considering Tier 3 within a response-to-intervention model. Accessed at www.rtinetwork.org/essential/tieredinstruction/tier3/ consideringtier3 on July 28, 2010.

Finn, J. D. (1982). Patterns in special education placement as revealed by the OCR surveys. In K. A. Heller, W. H. Holtzman, and S. Messick (Eds.), *Placing children in special education: A strategy for equity* (pp. 322–381). Washington, DC: National Academies Press.

Fisherman, J. (1989). *Language and ethnicity in minority sociolinguistic perspective.* Clevedon, England: Multilingual Matters.

Fletcher, J. M. (2007, February). *Overview of the Texas Center for Learning Disabilities.* Presentation at the Pacific Coast Research Conference, San Diego, CA.

Fletcher, J. M. (n.d.). *Identifying learning disabilities in the context of response to intervention: A hybrid model.* Accessed at www .rtinetwork.org/Learn/LD/ar/HybridModel on April 30, 2010.

Fletcher, J. M., Denton, C.A., Fuchs, L., & Vaughn, S. R. (2005). Multi-tiered reading instruction: Linking general education and special education. In S. Richardson & J. W. Gilger (Eds.), *Research-based education and intervention: What we need to know* (pp. 21–43). Baltimore: International Dyslexia Association.

Fletcher, J. M., Lyon, G. R., Barnes, M., Stuebing, K. K., Francis, D. J., et al. (n.d.). *Classification of learning disabilities: An evidence-based evaluation.* Accessed at www.nrcld.org/resources/ ldsummit/fletcher2.html on April 30, 2010.

Fuchs, D., Compton, D. L., Fuchs, L. S., Bryant, J. D., & Davis, G. N. (in press). Making "secondary intervention" work in a three-tier responsiveness-to-intervention model: Findings from the first-grade longitudinal reading study at the National Research Center on Learning Disabilities. *Reading and Writing: An Interdisciplinary Journal.*

Fuchs, D., & Fuchs, L. (2005). Peer-assisted learning strategies: Promoting word recognition, fluency, and reading comprehension in young children. *Journal of Special Education, 39*(1), 34–44.

Fuchs, D., Mock, D., Morgan, P., & Young, C. (2003). Responsiveness-to-intervention: Definitions, evidence, and implications for the learning disabilities construct. *Learning Disabilities Research and Practice, 18*(3), 157–171.

Fuchs, D., Vaughn, S. R., & Fuchs, L. S. (Eds.). (in press). *Responsiveness to intervention.* Newark, DE: International Reading Association.

Fuchs, L. S., Fuchs, D., Hosp, M. K., & Jenkins, J. R. (2001). Oral reading fluency as an indicator of reading competence: A theoretical, empirical, and historical analysis. *Scientific Studies of Reading, 5*(3), 241–258.

Fuchs, L. S., Fuchs, D., & Maxwell, L. (2006). The validity of informal reading comprehension measures. *Remedial and Special Education, 9*(2), 20–28.

Gay, G. (2002). Preparing for culturally responsive teaching. *Journal of Teacher Education, 4*(2), 106–116.

Goldberg, E. (2001). *The executive brain: Frontal lobes and the civilized mind.* New York: Oxford University Press.

Good, R. H., Gruba, J., & Kaminski, R. A. (2002). Best practices in using Dynamic Indicators of Basic Early Literacy Skills (DIBELS) in an outcomes-driven model. In A. Thomas & J. Grimes (Eds.), *Best practices in school psychology IV* (pp. 699–720). Bethesda, MD: National Association of School Psychologists.

Greenfield, P. M., Brazelton, T. B., & Childs, C. P. (1989). From birth to maturity in Zinacantan: Ontogenesis in cultural context. In V. R. Bricker and G. H. Gossen (Eds.), *Ethnographic encounters in southern Mesoamerica: Essays in honor of Evon Zartman Vogt, Jr.* (pp. 177–216). Albany: Institute of Mesoamerican Studies, University at Albany, State University of New York.

Hall, S. (2009a). *Create your implementation blueprint: Stage 1—Exploration.* Accessed at www.rtinetwork.org/GetStarted/Develop/ar/Create-Your-Implementation-Blueprint-Stage-1-Exploration on June 14, 2010.

Hall, S. (2009b). *Create your implementation blueprint: Stage 2—Installation.* Accessed at www.rtinetwork.org/GetStarted/Develop/ar/Create-Your-Implementation-Blueprint-Stage-2-Installation on June 14, 2010.

Hall, S. (2009c). *Create your implementation blueprint: Introduction.* Accessed at www.rtinetwork.org/GetStarted/Develop/ar/Create-Your-Implementation-Blueprint on May 13, 2010.

Hasbrouck, J., & Tindal, G. (2006). Oral reading fluency norms: A valuable assessment tool for reading teachers. *The Reading Teacher, 59*(7), 636–644.

Hofstede, G. (1983, January). National cultures revisited. *Cross-Cultural Research, 18*(4), 285–305.

Hosp, J. L. (2009). *Response to intervention and the disproportionate representation of culturally and linguistically diverse students in special education.* Accessed at www.rtinetwork.org/Learn/Diversity/ar/DisproportionateRepresentation on April 7, 2009.

Hosp, M. K., & Fuchs, L. S. (2005). Using CBM as an indicator of decoding, word reading, and comprehension: Do the relations change with grade? *School Psychology Review, 34*(1), 9–26.

Hosp, J. L., & Reschly, D. J. (2003, August). Referral rates for intervention or assessment: A meta-analysis of racial differences. *Journal of Special Education, 37*(2), 67–80.

Howell, K. W., & Nolet, V. (2000). *Curriculum-based evaluation: Teaching and decision making* (3rd ed.). Belmont, CA: Wadsworth/ Thomson Learning.

IDEA Partnership. (n.d.). *Identification of specific learning disabilities.* Accessed at www.ideapartnership.org/index.php ?option=com_content&view= article&id=422:identification -of-specific-learning-disabilities-regulations&catid=30:idea-2004-regulatory-provisions& Itemid=58 on July 27, 2010.

IDEA Partnership. (2007a, July). *Leaving no child behind: Response to intervention.* Accessed at www.ideapartnership.org/ documents/RTI-intro-presenter-guide-7–30–07.pdf on June 15, 2009.

IDEA Partnership. (2007b, July). *Response to intervention: Policy considerations and implementation.* [Presenter's guide.] Accessed at http://ideapartnership.org/media/documents/RTI -Collection/intermediate/rti-intermediate-presenter-guide. pdf on April 26, 2010.

IDEA Partnership. (2007c, July). *Response to intervention and SLD identification.* [Presenter's guide.] Accessed at www.ideapartnership .org/documents/RTI-advanced-presenter-guide-7-30-07.pdf on April 26, 2010.

IDEA Partnership. (2007d, July). *Alignment with No Child Left Behind (NCLB) Act.* Accessed at www.ideapartnership.org/index .php?option=com_content&view=article&id=1344&osepp age=1 on April 26, 2010.

Individuals with Disabilities Education Act of 1990.

Individuals with Disabilities Education Act of 1997, Pub. L. No. 105-17, 111 Stat. 37 (1997).

Individuals with Disabilities Education Improvement Act of 2004 (2004). Federal Register 71, pp. 46539–46845. Accessed at www.ed.gov/policy/speced/guid/idea2004.html on February 25, 2009.

Individuals with Disabilities Education Improvement Act of 2004, Pub. L. No. 108-446, 118 Stat. 2647 (2005).

IRIS Center. (2007a). *Dialogue guides: Topic—Comparison of RTI approaches.* Accessed at http://ideapartnership.org/media/documents/RTI-Collection/beginning/iris_dg_2approach_rti.pdf on May 28, 2010.

IRIS Center. (2007b). *Dialogue guides: Topic—Struggling readers.* Accessed at http://ideapartnership.org/media/documents/RTI-Collection/ beginning/iris_dg_strugread_rti.pdf on March 25, 2010.

IRIS Center. (2007c). *Dialogue guides: Topic—Two approaches to response to intervention (RTI).* Accessed at http://ideapartnership.org/media/documents/RTI-Collection/beginning/iris_dg_2approach_rti.pdf on May 17, 2010.

Jensen, E. (2000, April). *The brain and learning.* Workshop, Dallas, TX.

Jensen, E. (2003). *Completing the puzzle.* Thousand Oaks, CA: Corwin Press.

Johnson, D. R., & Johnson, F. P. (2008). *Joining together: Group theory and group skills* (10th ed.). Upper Saddle River, NJ: Pearson.

Johnson, D. W., Johnson, R. T., & Holubec, E. J. (1998). *Cooperation in the classroom* (7th ed.). Edina, MN: Interaction Books.

Johnson, E., Mellard, D. F., Fuchs, D., & McKnight, M. A. (2006). *Responsiveness to intervention (RTI): How to do it.* Lawrence, KS: National Research Center on Learning Disabilities.

Kim, U., & Choi, S.-H. (1994). Individualism, collectivism, and child development: A Korean perspective. In P. M. Greenfield and R. R. Cocking (Eds.), *Cross-cultural roots of minority child development* (pp. 227–258). Hillsdale, NJ: Lawrence Erlbaum Associates.

Knappman, E. (Ed.). (1994). *Great American trials.* Detroit: Visible Ink Press.

Kovaleski, J. E. (2003, December). *The three tier model for identifying learning disabilities: Critical program features and system issues.* Paper presented at the National Research Center on Learning Disabilities Responsiveness-to-Intervention Symposium, Kansas City, MO. Accessed at http://nrcld.org/symposium2003/kovaleski/kovaleski3.html on October 12, 2009.

Kroesbergen, E. H., & van Luit, J. E. H. (2003). Mathematics interventions for children with special educational needs: A meta-analysis. *Remedial and Special Education, 24*(2), 97–114.

Kunjufu, J. (2005). *Keeping black boys out of special education.* Chicago: African American Images.

Lebra, T. S. (1994). Mother and child in a Japanese socialization: A Japan-U.S. comparison. In P. M. Greenfield and R. R. Cocking (Eds.), *Cross-cultural roots of minority child development* (pp. 259–274). Hillsdale, NJ: Lawrence Erlbaum Associates.

Lindsey, R. B., Robins, K. N., & Terrell, R. D. (2009). *Cultural proficiency: A manual for school leaders* (3rd ed.). Thousand Oaks, CA: Corwin Press.

Long, L. (2006). *Painless algebra* (2nd ed.). Hauppauge, NY: Barron's Educational Series.

Maanum, J. (2009). *The general educator's guide to special education.* Thousand Oaks, CA: Corwin Press.

Mangaliman, J. (2007, August 16). School test gap "not just economic": Poverty can't explain racial, ethnic divide. *San Jose Mercury News.*

Marzano, R. J. (1998, December). *A theory-based meta-analysis of research on instruction.* Aurora, CO: Mid-continent Regional Educational Laboratory.

Marzano, R. J. (2003). Direct vocabulary instruction: An idea whose time has come. In B. Williams (Ed.), *Closing the achievement gap: A vision for changing beliefs and practices* (2nd ed., pp. 48–66). Alexandria, VA: Association for Supervision and Curriculum Development.

Marzano, R. J. (2007). *The art and science of teaching: A comprehensive framework for effective instruction.* Alexandria, VA: Association for Supervision and Curriculum Development.

Marzano, R. J., & Kendall, J. S. (1996). *Designing standards-based districts, schools, and classrooms.* Alexandria, VA: Association for Supervision and Curriculum Development.

Marzano, R. J., & Pickering, D. J. (2005). *Building academic vocabulary: Teacher's manual.* Alexandria, VA: Association for Supervision and Curriculum Development.

McCray, A. D., Vaughn, S., & Neal, L. I. (2001). Not all students learn to read by third grade: Middle school students speak out about their reading disabilities. *Journal of Special Education, 35*(1), 17–30.

McMaster, K. L., Fuchs, D., & Fuchs, L. S. (2006). Research on peer-assisted learning strategies: The promise and limitations of peer-mediated instruction. *Reading & Writing Quarterly, 22*(1), 5–25.

Mid-continent Research for Education and Learning (McREL). (2003). *Sequenced benchmarks for K–12 for language arts.* Accessed at www.mcrel.org/PDF/Standards/5021TG_ELA _Sequenced_Bms.pdf#search=%22compendium%22 on March 5, 2010.

Mid-continent Research for Education and Learning (McREL). (2010). *List of benchmarks for language arts.* Accessed at www.mcrel.org/ compendium/standardDetails. asp?subjectID=7&standardID=5 on May 2, 2010.

Montague, M. (2007). Self-regulation and mathematics instruction. *Learning Disabilities Research and Practice, 22*(1), 75–83.

National Center for Learning Disabilities. (2010). *RTI Action Network: Glossary.* Accessed at www.rtinetwork.org/component/ option,com_glossary/Itemid,1/ on May 2, 2010.

National Reading Panel. (2000). *Teaching children to read: An evidence-based assessment of the scientific research literature on reading and its implications for reading instruction.* Washington, DC: U.S. Government Printing Office.

National Research Center on Learning Disabilities. (2007). *What is RTI?* Accessed at www.nrcld.org/topics/rti.html on April 27, 2010.

No Child Left Behind Act of 2001, 20 U.S.C. § 6301 *et seq.* (2002).

Northeast and Islands Regional Educational Laboratory at Brown University. (2002). *The diversity kit: An introductory resource for social change in education. Part II: Culture.* Providence, RI: Author.

O'Connell, J. (2008, January 22). *State of education address.* Presented at the California Department of Education Annual Address, Sacramento, CA. Accessed at www.cde.ca.gov/eo/in/se/yr08stateofed.asp on May 16, 2008.

Ogbu, J. U. (1992). Understanding cultural diversity and learning. *Educational Researcher, 21*(8), 5–14.

Osborne, A. G., Jr., & Russo, C. J. (2006). *Special education and the law: A guide for practitioners.* Thousand Oaks, CA: Corwin Press.

Parsad, B., Lewis, L., & Ferris, E. (2001). *Fast response.* Washington, DC: National Center for Education Statistics.

Payne, R. K. (2001). *A framework for understanding poverty.* Highlands, TX: aha! Process.

President's Commission on Excellence in Special Education. (2002). *A new era: Revitalizing special education for children and their families.* Accessed at www2.ed.gov/inits/commissionsboards/whspecialeducation/reports/index.html on April 27, 2010.

Pullen, P. C., Lane, H. B., Lloyd, J. W., Nowak, R., & Ryals, J. (2005). Effects of explicit instruction on decoding of struggling first grade students: A data-based case study. *Education and Treatment of Children, 28*(1), 63–76.

Saenz, L. M, Fuchs, L. S., & Fuchs, D. (2005). Peer-assisted learning strategies for English language learners with learning disabilities. *Exceptional Children, 71*(3), 231–247.

Scherer, M. (2007, October). Interventions that work: Early intervention at every age. *Educational Leadership, 65*(2), 7.

Shade, B. (1994). Understanding the African American learner. In E. R. Hollins, J. D. King, & W. C. Haymen (Eds.), *Teaching diverse populations: Formulating a new knowledge base* (pp. 175–189). Albany: State University of New York Press.

Shade, B. J., Kelly, C., & Oberg, M. (1997). *Creating culturally responsive classrooms.* Washington, DC: American Psychological Association.

Shaywitz, S. E. (2003). *Overcoming dyslexia: A manual and complete science-based program for reading problems at any level.* New York: Knopf.

Sheets, R. H. (2005). *Diversity pedagogy: Examining the role of culture in the teaching-learning process.* New York: Allyn & Bacon.

Sheets, R. H. (2008). *Diversity pedagogy: Examining the role of culture in the teaching-learning process.* New Jersey: Allyn & Bacon.

Small, M. F. (1998). *Our babies, ourselves: How biology and culture shape the way we parent.* New York: Anchor Books.

Sousa, D. A. (2001). *How the brain learns.* Thousand Oaks, CA: Corwin Press.

Sousa, D. A. (2005). *How the brain learns to read.* Thousand Oaks, CA: Corwin Press.

Sousa, D. A. (2008). *How the brain influences behavior: Management strategies for every classroom.* Thousand Oaks, CA: Corwin Press.

Suina, J. H., & Smolkin, L. B. (1994). From natal culture to school culture to dominant society culture: Supporting transitions for Pueblo Indian students. In P. M. Greenfield and R. R. Cocking (Eds.), *Cross-cultural roots of minority child development* (pp. 115–130). Hillsdale, NJ: Lawrence Erlbaum Associates.

Tileston, D. W. (2005). *What every teacher should know about learning, memory and the brain.* Thousand Oaks, CA: Corwin Press.

Tileston, D. W. (2010). *What every teacher should know about diverse learners* (2nd ed.). Thousand Oaks, CA: Corwin Press.

Tileston, D. W., & Darling, S. K. (2008). *Preparing students for high-stakes tests.* Thousand Oaks, CA: Corwin Press.

Tileston, D. W., & Darling, S. K. (2009). *Why culture counts: Teaching children of poverty.* Bloomington, IN: Solution Tree Press.

University of California, Berkeley. (2010). *Practices for the documentation and accommodation of students with attention-deficit/ hyperactivity disorder.* Accessed at http://dsp.berkeley.edu/ add.html on May 1, 2010.

U.S. Department of Education. (2000). *To assure the free appropriate public education of all children with disabilities.* Presented at the Twenty-Second Annual Report to Congress on the Implementation of the Individuals with Disabilities Education Act, Washington, DC.

U.S. Department of Education Office of Special Education and Rehabilitative Services. (2002, July 1). *A new era: Revitalizing special education for children and their families.* Accessed at www.ed.gov/inits/commissionsboards/whspecialeducation/ reports/index.html on September 20, 2008.

U.S. Department of Health and Human Services. (2001). *Mental health: Culture, race and ethnicity—A supplement to* Mental health: A report of the Surgeon General. Rockville, MD: U.S. Department of Health and Human Services, Public Health Service, Office of the Surgeon General.

U.S. Office of Education. (1968). *First annual report of the National Advisory Committee on Handicapped Children.* Washington, DC: U.S. Department of Health, Education, and Welfare.

Vaughn, S. (2003, December 4–5). *How many tiers are needed for response to intervention to achieve acceptable prevention outcomes?* Presented at the National Research Center on Learning Disabilities Responsiveness-to-Intervention Symposium, Kansas City, MO.

Vaughn, S., Cirino, P. T., Linan-Thompson, S., Mathes, P. G., Carlson, C. D., Cardenas-Hagan, E., et al. (2006). Effectiveness of a Spanish intervention and an English intervention for English language learners at risk for reading problems. *American Educational Research Journal, 43*(3), 449–487.

Villegas, A. M. (1991). *Culturally responsive pedagogy for the 1990's and beyond.* Princeton, NJ: Educational Testing Service.

Wenglinsky, H. (2002, February 13). How schools matter: The link between teacher classroom practices and student academic performance. *Education Policy Analysis Archives, 10*(12).

Accessed at http://epaa.asu.edu/epaa/v10n12 on May 5, 2003.

Wereschagin, M. (2007). Pittsburgh study: Teachers key in affecting pupils' success. *Pittsburgh Tribune-Review.* Accessed at www .pittsburghlive.com/x/pittsburghtrib/?source=network+bar on September 11, 2007.

Williams, B. (Ed.). (2003). *Closing the achievement gap: A vision for changing beliefs and practices* (2nd ed.). Alexandria, VA: Association for Supervision and Curriculum Development.

Witt, J. C., VanDerHeyden, A. M., & Gilbertson, D. (2004). Trouble-shooting behavioral interventions: A systematic process for finding and eliminating problems. *School Psychology Review, 33*(3), 363–383.

Wright, J. (2006, January). *Getting started with "response to intervention": A guide for schools.* Accessed at www.jimwrightonline .com/ppt/rti_intro_wright.ppt#257 on April 27, 2010.

Yopp, H. K., & Yopp, R. H. (2000). Supporting phonemic awareness development in the classroom. *The Reading Teacher, 54*(2), 130–143.

Zaner-Bloser. (2003). *Should bugs bug you.* Columbus, OH: Author.

Ziegler, B. M. (Ed.). (1958). *Desegregation and the Supreme Court* Boston: D.C. Heath.

Index

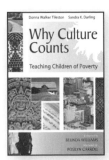

Why Culture Counts: Teaching Children of Poverty
Donna Walker Tileston and Sandra K. Darling
Foreword by Belinda Williams
Afterword by Rosilyn Carroll
Learn how to use students' cultural assets to close the achievement gap with these research-based methods of differentiating the context, content, and process of instruction. **BKF255**

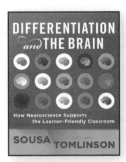

Differentiation and the Brain
David A. Sousa and Carol Ann Tomlinson
Examine the basic principles of differentiation in light of educational neuroscience research that will help you make the most effective curricular, instructional, and assessment choices. **BKF353**

Beyond the RTI Pyramid
Solutions for the First Years of Implementation
William N. Bender
This book helps schools deepen the RTI experience by extending the processes beyond initial implementation and across various content areas and grade levels. **BKF323**

Boys in Poverty
A Framework for Understanding Dropout
Ruby K. Payne and Paul D. Slocumb
Foreword by Michael Gurian
Examine risks and interventions for dropout among boys in poverty. Explore dropout among sensitive, gay, gifted, ADHD, and postadolescent males. **BKF383**

Solution Tree | Press

a division of
Solution Tree

Visit solution-tree.com or call 800.733.6786 to order.

Solution Tree | Press

a division of
Solution Tree

Solution Tree's mission is to advance the work of our authors. By working with the best researchers and educators worldwide, we strive to be the premier provider of innovative publishing, in-demand events, and inspired professional development designed to transform education to ensure that all students learn.

The mission of the National Association of Elementary School Principals is to lead in the advocacy and support for elementary and middle level principals and other education leaders in their commitment for all children.